praise for sexual morality in a Christless world

In an age of compromise, it is refreshing to read a work that takes a firm stand on a controversial topic. This book is both faithful to Scripture and pastoral in its approach. Although the sin of homosexuality is clearly described as contrary to God's will, the presentation of the Gospel is applied clearly and powerfully in a way that should bring comfort and hope to the repentant. I pray that it will be widely read. It will offer clarity to many who want to believe the truth but don't always know how to defend it.

—Rev. Daniel Preus, DD
Third Vice President, The Lutheran Church—Missouri Synod
President of the Luther Academy Board of Directors

The long run of conservative morality in this country that has been shaped by Christian ethics is coming to an end. In a wonderful, biblically faithful way, Rueger shows what it means to be a confessing Christian in the twenty-first century as he turns our attention to the bold witness of the first-century Christians who stood out among a promiscuous society and turned the world to the Gospel. This book will help those suffering under sexual confusion with a biblical sexual morality that is both compassionate and Christ-centered.

—Rev. Gary W. Zieroth, DMin
Senior Pastor, St. John's Lutheran Church and School, Chaska, MN
Adjunct Professor, Concordia Theological Seminary, Fort Wayne, IN
Interim Director, PALS (Post-Seminary Applied Learning and Support)

We live in a world where traditional views on sexuality and marriage are collapsing. How do we stand up for a Christian position when it is rejected simply because it is Christian? Dr. Rueger uses Scriptures and early Christianity to show that we are not alone, nor is there anything new under the sun. His discussions are thoughtful and clear, compassionate and Christ-centered. Biblical sexual morality will always be countercultural. This book is a helpful, welcome apologetic.

—Deaconess Sandra Rhein
Hymnal Consultant, LCMS Office of International Missions
Deaconess, Emmaus Lutheran Church, South Bend, IN

Against all odds, this timely book offers a beautiful contribution to the ongoing challenge of sexual morality. At a point when many of us are tired of hearing about it, Dr. Rueger has managed to engage the topic in a gently compelling way. He has written elegantly about a decidedly inelegant subject, demonstrating enviable dignity and a gracious decorum throughout. His firsthand participation in the public debate has evidently served him well. His arguments are well organized, thoroughly developed, and consistently evangelical. He is faithful in bringing both the Law and the Gospel to bear, and in his cogent use of reason and sound logic. I honestly did not expect to enjoy this book, but was surprised to find how pleasant and encouraging it is.

—Rev. D. Richard Stuckwisch, PhD
Pastor, Emmaus Evangelical Lutheran Church, South Bend, IN

Matthew Rueger reminds us that wider social opposition to Christian sexual morality is no recent, contemporary development. Christians have been mocked and sanctioned to varying degrees for their opposition to social sex practices since the first century. Their courage encourages us today to remain resolute with Scriptural testimony—even when we might be mocked or sanctioned—not for the sake of culture wars or condemnation of others, but to continue to set forth the new life in Christ. Rueger calls for steadfastness in the face of increasing social opposition while offering deeply-reasoned pastoral insights to serve repentance from immorality, reconciliation with God, and healing in the Spirit.

—Rev. Gifford Grobien, PhD
Assistant Professor of Systematic Theology
Director of DMin Program
Concordia Theological Seminary, Fort Wayne, IN

"The world's goin' to hell in a handbasket!" So lament many modern Christians, surrounded by confusing ethical issues of our day. While believers in Christ may be tempted to throw up their hands in an increasingly challenging social context, we have hope. This hope is clearly and compellingly laid out in Matthew Rueger's excellent book.

Instead of hand-wringing, Rueger gives advice for remaining true to the Christian witness. Not only does he present a Christian perspective on many sexual ethical issues; he does so by providing a clear contextual, historical, and biblical background in a way that provides hope and guidance for modern Christians. It is scholarly and yet accessible to an average reader. This book would be a terrific resource for adult Bible classes, or for older teens and parents to provide discussion material for navigating the moral and biblical questions of our time.

—Professor Scott and Julie Stiegemeyer
Authors of *Your Marriage by God's Design* (CPH, 2014)

Sexual Morality in a Christless World

matthew rueger

Peer Reviewed

CONCORDIA PUBLISHING HOUSE • SAINT LOUIS

Published by Concordia Publishing House
3558 S. Jefferson Ave., St. Louis, MO 63118-3968
1-800-325-3040 • www.cph.org
Copyright © 2016 Matthew Rueger

Cover photo ©iStockPhoto.com

Manufactured in the United States of America

Library of Congress Cataloging-in-Publication Data

Names: Rueger, Matthew, author.

Title: Sexual morality in a Christless world / Matthew Rueger.

Description: St. Louis : Concordia Publishing House, 2016.

Identifiers: LCCN 2016008224 (print) | LCCN 2016009125 (ebook) | ISBN 9780758656384 | ISBN 9780758656391 ()

Subjects: LCSH: Sex--Religious aspects--Christianity.

Classification: LCC BT708 .R84 2016 (print) | LCC BT708 (ebook) | DDC 241/.664--dc23

LC record available at http://lccn.loc.gov/2016008224

1 2 3 4 5 6 7 8 9 10   25 24 23 22 21 20 19 18 17 16

Table of Contents

INTRODUCTION

During the fall semester of 2010, my future son-in-law, Ryan, was attending an ethics class at Iowa State University. His professor's teaching method pushed students to reassess accepted views on ethics, morality, and politics. On one particular weekend, when Ryan came to visit my daughter, I heard him complain about how sexual ethics were being presented in this class. It frustrated him that other students were taught to see sexuality in humanistic terms where sexual morality was an open question. Ryan felt that Christian standards of sexual morality were being presented as outdated and largely irrelevant. That certainly was not limited to the ethics classroom. At that time, outside one of the university cafeterias every Wednesday, a table was set up offering free condoms right across from another table bearing a sign that read "Ask an Atheist," which was manned by an atheist ready to debunk irrational religious ideas. Among the many student organizations offered at the university was a club called "Cuffs" that advertised itself as a group that met for discussion and education. Among the topics of interest discussed are BDSM (which includes: Bondage and Discipline, Dominance and Submission, Sadism and Masochism), fetishes, and "alternative sexuality."[1] It was nicknamed the "orgy club" by some of the students. I suspect that the sexual hedonism witnessed by Ryan is typical of most secular university campuses. His disappointment and frustration with such immorality is felt by scores of Christian students.

I shared Ryan's frustration, and as we talked, I searched for something to say to make him feel like all was not lost. I finally suggested that he should stay after class and voice his concerns to the professor. Not really thinking Ryan would actually do it, I suggested that he approach the professor saying that in the spirit of academic freedom, a speaker should be brought in who could present sexual ethics from a conservative point of view. That way the students would have an opportunity to see firsthand how both sides of the debate shape their ethical arguments.

---

[1] Iowa State University Student Organization Database, www.stuorg.iastate.edu/site/cuffs (accessed January 21, 2016).

Ryan is a very quiet young man and not the type to be verbally confrontational, but he must have been more upset than I knew, because much to my surprise, Ryan did go to his professor and pass on my suggestion; and then even more to my surprise, the professor agreed! I do not know exactly how the conversation progressed after that, but somehow Ryan suggested me as the counterpoint to the professor and the professor again agreed.

The professor emailed me and asked specifically that I address homosexuality and same-sex marriage, not just from a conservative point of view, but from a Christian perspective. Suddenly, I found myself having to prepare a reasoned presentation on sexual ethics for a secular university classroom that I knew would be hostile to my point of view. A year before this, the Iowa Supreme Court legalized same-sex marriage, so the topic was a hot one on university campuses throughout Iowa.

My first presentation was all the more exciting inasmuch as it followed gay pride week at Iowa State. Much to the credit of this professor, he allowed me to make my case without interruption. He also seemed to have been pleased by the way the presentation went because he asked me to return in following semesters to give the same lecture to his classes. The professor began each lecture by introducing me and telling his class to be respectful but "go after him." They were not shy about fulfilling his wishes. Some students got angry. Some got up and left the room, letting the door slam behind them for effect. Others considered it their duty to debate me while citing articles on their smartphones. Usually one or two students stayed after the lecture and thanked me for giving voice to what they believed but were afraid to say for fear of retaliation. The experience opened my eyes to the ethical perspectives on secular university campuses. It is from my work preparing for these lectures that this volume was born.

Within recent years, the topic of homosexual rights and same-sex "marriage" has exploded. The rhetoric has become downright vicious. There is such resistance to open, reasoned, discussion that it is nearly impossible to engage in a public debate about the morality of homosexuality without being personally attacked. Sadly, the rhetoric cuts both ways. Not only are those who oppose the pro-homosexual agenda demonized, but those in favor of gay rights are often shouted down and attacked by Bible-thumping bullies. The emotional baggage brought to the debate becomes vitriolic to the point of preventing reasoned dialogue.

My desire in writing this book is to help Christians engage the world around them in reasoned discussion. I also write as a father wishing to help my children when they get dragged into debates. My wife and I have been blessed with seven children, five of which are in the university as I begin writing this. They regularly tell me about conversations they have with friends and classmates. Often they find themselves facing a group of angry peers who are more interested in shouting them down than discussing the ethics of homosexuality versus heterosexuality.

It is painful as a parent to watch your kids be treated with contempt, but we now live in an era where Christians must expect unpleasant confrontations. This is nothing new of course; the ethics of sexuality presented in the New Testament have always been both countercultural and radical. Christianity has always raised the ire of the secular status quo. A common accusation made against Christians is that biblical sexual ethics does nothing more than cling to old fashioned traditionalism; "Christians are just holding onto the past and aren't willing to change." As will be shown, this accusation is as ironic as it is wrong. Christian views on sexual morality were departures from older established traditions, Roman and Jewish.

When St. Paul wrote his letters to the Romans, Ephesians, and Corinthians, he was not calling on new converts to return to old traditions. He was instead calling on them to break with tradition, to dare to take a stand and admit the culture around them was wrong. Paul made it personal; he urged them to admit that they, too, had erred in the past by following cultural traditions that were out of step with God's will. With Christ came a new way of living, a different way of thinking and acting. Paul did not weigh public opinion to see if the new Christian morality would be accepted. He knew it would not be.

Such a bold confession put Christians at odds with anyone who kept to the older cultural ways. In particular, it earned Christians the deep abiding hatred of the Roman government. Sexual promiscuity, homosexuality, intercourse between adults and adolescents, prostitution and rape were not only legal, they were part and parcel of the cultural norm. What many "progressives" today fail to understand is that the attitudes about sexuality they champion (a.k.a. open hedonism) are in reality the practices and cultural norms of societies like Rome that predate Christ's birth. Ironically, they, and not Christians, are looking to return to ancient traditional standards.

When Paul brought Christianity to Rome, promiscuity was seen as a positive element in the economic life of Roman cities. In a keynote address to the Fourth Biennial Dignity International Convention, John Boswell, a professor at Yale University, claimed that male prostitution (directed toward other males) was not only taxed in ancient Rome but the amount of tax collected was a significant portion of the royal treasury.[2] Local governments depended on the sex trade. The Romans tended to be very open about their sexual exploits. Senators were known to brag in public speeches about their sexual attraction for the young men with whom they were involved. When Christians turned away from Roman sex practices, they were, in effect, calling the entire ethical system of their culture into question.

Unlike St. Paul in Rome, we have enjoyed a long run of conservative morality in this country that has been sympathetic to, if not outright shaped by, Christian ethics. Our grandparents did not have to fight against the acceptance of immorality as our children do today. When talking to one of my parishioners who recently retired, he said he had never even heard about homosexuality until he was a junior or senior in high school, and then he did not believe it was real. Thirty-five years ago, when I was in high school, there was one student who was rumored to be homosexual, and that was in a high school of about six hundred. Now my kids go to school dances and watch lesbians "making out" on the dance floor. In their high school of about 240 students, there are eight or more boys and girls either openly homosexual or claiming to be bisexual.

The world has changed and now we Christians find ourselves increasingly in the position of the Christians in St. Paul's day as outcasts and radicals. Will we mirror the ancient Christians who were not afraid to stand out in the crowd and say, "Not for me?" Are we willing to be ostracized, excluded, secretly derided, and maybe even openly mocked simply because we are Christians? We need to be; our children need to be. The younger generation more than the adults are on the front lines with this issue, and it is they who will be forced to stand against authority figures in school and say, "That's not what God wants." Before they can make such a stand and present a clear case for their position, they need to

---

[2] John Boswell, "The Church and the Homosexual: An Historical Perspective 1979," Excerpts from the keynote address to the Fourth Biennial Dignity International Convention in 1979, Fordham University, legacy.fordham.edu/halsall/pwh/1979boswell.asp (accessed January 21, 2016).

know why as Christians their morality is God pleasing and why they need not be ashamed to speak about it in public.

The challenges that Christians face in the secular world will not be limited to secular venues. As society grows more comfortable with forcing its moral vision on those who disagree, Christians will find the fight creeping into the peaceful sanctuary of their churches. It is not at all unreasonable to imagine a scenario where current anti-discrimination or hate-crime laws will be used against churches to force them to perform same-sex marriages or hire pastors regardless of sexual orientation. There may come a time when congregations lose their tax exempt status if they refuse to adopt accepted secular morality. Pastors may face fines and prison time if they publicly condemn homosexuality.

Clashes between the world and Christians over sexual morality go back to the very first Christian communities. Christians today can better prepare themselves to give an answer to those who disagree by looking to the examples of our ancient forefathers and foremothers. In chapters 1 and 2, the reader will be introduced to the sexual climate in the world of the early Christians. Roman perspectives on sex exerted enormous pressure on early Christians as did rabbinical Jewish traditions about sex and marriage. Christian attitudes took shape in the midst of these divergent cultural views. Chapter 3 will explore specific Bible passages that guided Christian thought and practice. Knowing what the apostles said and in what context they said it is a necessary foundation for any discussion about sexual ethics that are genuinely Christian. In chapter 4, the focus changes; where early chapters aim primarily at helping Christians understand the roots of Christian sexual ethics, chapter 4 focuses on how this affects real people today. Debate and reasoned discussion with the secular world must exemplify the best Christian compassion with those suffering under sexual confusion. This chapter will discuss how biblical sexual morality is both compassionate and Christ-centered. Chapter 5 faces common secular objections to Christian teachings about sex. Knowing the objections of one's opponents can be helpful in shaping a coherent answer to their complaints. The final chapter offers a possible avenue of debate that may prove helpful with those who reject the Christian position simply because it is Christian.

chapter 1

The Roman Context

I am a pastor, and in the seminary we were taught that one of the main principles of biblical interpretation is that context determines meaning. A person can make the Bible say whatever he or she wants it to say if words or phrases are pulled out of their context. Most times, context involves looking at the verses around a particular passage in question. It means asking, "What is the overall message of this whole section?" Determining context may also involve looking at the other writings of that same author or examining the whole of Scripture to see what the overarching teaching of Christianity is on the subject. Understanding context demands considering the world in which this or that text was written. What would that passage mean to the people to whom it was originally written? A great deal of biblical scholarship has focused on researching the historical context of Scripture.

Because the New Testament was written within the milieu of first century Judaism, it is not surprising that a lot of research has been devoted to exploring first century Jewish culture. Jesus was obviously Jewish and ministered within Jewish communities; so if we want to know about His life and the world in which He lived, we need to dig into the customs, practices, and faith of the Jewish people in His day. Indeed, such contextual research has yielded good fruit in understanding the meaning of many of Jesus' teachings.

When the discussion turns to sexual ethics and the New Testament, though, a context that needs more scholarly attention is first century Roman culture. Nearly all of the texts dealing with sexuality were written to people living within Roman, not Jewish, cities. Since this book spends

11

a great deal of time addressing the issue of homosexuality, we note that the Jews did not approve of homosexual behavior. The Old Testament condemns homosexual activity in strong terms, and the Jewish people in the apostolic age would have been repulsed by homosexuality. There was little need to lay out a case against homosexuality to the Jews. The Romans, on the other hand, had no scruples about homosexual behavior, as will be shown.

If one were to overlay a map showing the missionary travels of St. Paul with a map of the Roman Empire in the first century, it could be seen that every city where Paul went was part of the Roman Empire. Every city named in his letters was Roman. Cities like Ephesus, Corinth, Thessalonica, Galatia, and Rome were governed by Roman law and Roman morality. Yes, many of these cities had roots going back centuries into Greek culture, but by Paul's day, all were "Romanized." Paul brought Christian teaching to a people whose present and ancient morality was hostile to Christianity. In both ancient Greek and first century Roman culture, homosexual behavior between males was understood as completely normal. Paul knew what he said about sexuality would be counter-cultural.

The old morality against which St. Paul stood dated back a thousand years or more. In the pages following, it is my intent to paint a more detailed picture of what the moral climate was like when St. Paul taught God's Word to the Gentile converts. This context is essential to grasp because in many regards, Rome's sexual climate is a model of the utopia for which today's sexual "progressives" are striving. If Christians wish to bear witness to the truth of Christ in today's circumstances, then understanding the struggles of first century Christians living within the context of the Roman Empire will prove helpful.

sexual orientation

The apparent universal acceptance of the idea that someone is "oriented" toward a specific gender is a modern phenomenon. Often, the world divides people into those who are oriented toward the opposite sex (heterosexuals), those who are oriented toward the same sex (homosexuals), and those whose orientation includes either sex (bisexuals or pansexuals). Orientation implies that sexual preference is set by nature and is beyond one's control. This understanding was exemplified by the Iowa Supreme Court when it issued its decision legalizing same sex marriage in 2009. The court claimed that one's sexual orientation is "immutable"—that is, it is an essential part of one's nature and "may be altered [if at all] only at the expense of significant damage to the individual's sense of self."[1]

Later in this volume, a separate section will be devoted to the issue of "immutability" or being "born that way."[2] For now, this matter is raised only to demonstrate the fact that orientation is a legally recognized means of speaking of sexuality. It is simply a given in our culture that people are oriented toward one kind of sexuality—hetero, homo, or bi.

The ancient world of the Greeks and Romans did not understand sexuality in terms of orientation. Some authors have claimed that the first notions of orientation can be found in later Roman thinking (second and third century),[3] yet from the evidence supplied, this was a minority opinion that hardly ever entered into the public conversation.

Sexuality went beyond orientation. For the Greek world, sex was about the pursuit of beauty. Greeks were captivated by the beauty of the young male form. It is no accident that the Greek god of love, Eros (from which we get the word *erotic*), was portrayed as a young boy. The Roman counterpart to Eros was Cupid (from the Latin "Cupido" or "desire"), a deity also pictured as a young boy. Ancient Greek texts are full of references to the pursuit of homosexual intercourse with boys because their beauty was the most striking to the eye.

The Romans at first seemed to consider this Greek obsession with the beauty of boys a cause of weakness. Roman sexuality was different than Greek. It was tied more to ideas of masculinity and the Roman male's need for domination. That being said, there are still many ancient manuscripts showing how Romans continued to obsess over male beauty and sexuality. Plutarch (late first to early second century AD) gives expression to this: "The noble lover of beauty engages in love wherever he sees excellence and splendid natural endowment without regard for any difference in physiological detail."[4]

---

[1] Varnum v. Brien, No. 07–1499, IA, 44 (April 2009).

[2] Cf. pp. 113ff. and 135ff.

[3] Thomas K. Hubbard, *Homosexuality in Greece and Rome* (Los Angeles: University of California Press, 2003), 444.

[4] Plutarch, *Moralia*, Volume IX, trans. by Edwin L. Minar Jr., F. H. Sandbach, W. C. Helmbold in Loeb Classical Library Volume 425 (Cambridge, MA: Harvard University Press, 1961), 415. Copyright © 1961 by the President and Fellows of Harvard College. Loeb

In the Roman mind, the strong took what they wanted to take. It was socially acceptable for a strong Roman male to have intercourse with men or women alike, provided he was the aggressor. It was looked down upon to play the female "receptive" role in homosexual liaisons. However, even that was allowed provided the man had proven his strength in other areas. For instance, Julius Caesar was well-known to have "played the woman" with Nicomede, the king of Bithynia. Soldiers returning from Gaul even sang songs about it: "The Gauls to Caesar yield, Caesar to Nicomede, Lo! Caesar triumphs for his glorious deed, but Caesar's conqueror gains no victor's mead."[5] Julius Caesar's sexual exploits were so well-known that a public orator said that Julius is "Every woman's man and every man's woman."[6] Despite the raised eyebrows with Julius playing the woman in sexual encounters with men, he was given a pass by society because he proved his strength and manliness through his many military conquests.

Because of the worship of manly strength, it was acceptable for a man to have sex with his slaves, male or female. It was understood that he would be visiting prostitutes of either sex. A strong Roman male would have male lovers even while married to a woman. In the Roman mind, man was the conqueror who dominated on the battlefield as well as in the bedroom. He was strong, muscular, and hard in both body and spirit. Society looked down on him only when he appeared weak or soft. Being the receiver of a sex act was considered feminine and therefore soft or weak. The very language used to describe men given to homosexuality and a word St. Paul himself used in 1 Corinthians 6 is *malakos*, which means "soft."

This attitude toward male strength shaped Roman views about rape. Rape, by and large, was prosecutable only if it involved free Roman citizens. The penalties tended to be monetary fines, not imprisonment or death. The Caesars, who were the icons of Roman strength, lived above legal repercussions for their sexual conquests. The Caesars are known to have had intercourse with the wives of senators and other highly placed public figures without civil penalties. Augustus is said to have used this as

---

Classical Library® is a registered trademark of the President and Fellows of Harvard College.

[5] Suetonius, *Lives of the Twelve Caesars*, trans. Alexander Thomson, rev. by T. Forester (London: George Bell and Sons, 1890), 33.

[6] Suetonius, *Lives of the Twelve Caesars*, 34.

a means of uncovering plots against him by the husbands of the women with whom he slept.[7]

pederasty

This pursuit of beauty and maintaining of the masculine ideal led to a deeply pervasive institution in Greek and later Roman culture called pederasty. Pederasty is a sexual relationship between an adult man and an adolescent boy. This was no flash-in-the-pan moral blip that came and went. This was a thousand-year-old social institution that enjoyed complete acceptance by Greek and Roman society.

In his book *Roman Homosexuality*, Craig Williams identifies a difference between Greek and Roman pederasty.[8] While the Greeks made no distinction between citizen and noncitizens in such relationships, it was, at least in the early years of the Republic, a taboo for Roman men to pursue pederast relations with freeborn boys. Freeborn boys were Roman citizens and were also potential leaders in Roman society. They were to be treated with more respect and held more legal rights than those not born free Roman citizens. However, taboo or not, the practice of Roman sexual relations with freeborn boys is well-documented. What was not taboo, but a common expectation, was Roman pederasty directed at young male slaves.

If a Greek man were to describe pederasty, he would justify it as a normal part of a boy's overall education and as positive means of advancement for a youth. He would see the role of the adult male as teacher. The teacher would train the youth in matters of culture, language, social expectations, ideals of manliness, and of course, sex. Roman culture put less stress on the cultural/educational aspect of pederasty and tended to pursue it more on grounds of fulfilling one's manly desire— which made no differentiation between male or female. It was not uncommon for a Roman man to expend large amounts of money on his boy, plying him with gifts and rewarding him for various achievements. Slave boys who won the sexual affection of their masters may be set free when they matured.

---

[7] Suetonius, *Lives of the Twelve Caesars*, 122.

[8] Craig A Williams, *Roman Homosexuality* (New York: Oxford University Press, 1999), 62–64.

At the end of the day, however, regardless of any educational, social, or financial benefits, the boy was being raped. He was raped repeatedly over the course of several years with his and his family's permission. This "love affair" between a man and his boy was praised as one of deep affection and devotion. Many ancient poems and works of prose exist where the man swoons at his sexual desire for his boy. The pederast relationship did not end until the boy reached adulthood and began to grow facial and body hair. To delay the maturation process and keep his youthful looks, his body hair might be plucked out or otherwise depilated. In the case of slaves, he might be castrated.

For a thousand years, pederasty was the norm. More than the norm, in many circles it was actually considered the purest form of love. In both the Greek and Roman mind, the relationship between man and woman in marriage was not a union of equals. A man's wife was often seen as beneath him and less than him, but a sexual relationship with another male, boy or man, represented a higher form of intellectual love and engagement. It was a man joining with that which was his equal and who could therefore share experiences and ideas with him in a way he could not with a woman.

There was a serious contradiction in the psychology of Roman sexuality. On the one hand, there were no scruples about men having intercourse with other men (usually young men or boys). Homosexual behavior was accepted by the vast majority of Romans. On the other hand, there were issues for the Romans with being on the receiving side of that homoerotic union. The receiver was looked down upon as weak and soft. He was becoming the woman in the sexual relationship and therefore was not the ideal Roman aggressor. In pederasty, boys who were being "educated" to become the Roman ideal of strength and virility were expected to be the receiver of the adult man's sexual advances. It was excused on the basis that an adolescent boy was not yet a man and therefore was more soft and womanly in physical form. But still, it was against the stated purpose of shaping the ideal Roman male to expect the boy to play the woman.

To ease consciences with regard to this apparent contradiction, it was expected of the boy that he show some resistance. He was to refuse his adult male courtier for a time and allow himself to be pursued and bribed with gifts. If he was too willing, then his manhood could be called into question. This desire of preserving potential manhood in boys by expecting them to resist predates the Roman Empire in which St. Paul lived. A historian named Ephorus of Cyme (fourth century BC) recorded how on Crete there was a practice of ritualistic abduction of young boys. By ritualistically abducting boys, even with a mock show of resistance, boys could claim they were not willing and therefore were not womanly. Ephorus writes:

> They have a peculiar custom in regard to love affairs, for they win the objects of their love, not by persuasion, but by abduction; the lover tells the friends of the boy three or four days beforehand that he is going to make the abduction; but for the friends to conceal the boy, or not to let him go forth by the appointed road, is indeed a most disgraceful thing, a confession, as it were, that the boy is unworthy to obtain such a lover; and when they meet, if the abductor is the boy's equal or superior in rank or other respects, the friends pursue him and lay hold of him, though only in a very gentle way, thus satisfying the custom; and after that they cheerfully turn the boy over to him to lead away.[9]

While I am no psychologist, there does seem to be something akin to pathological behavior at work here. There is tacit admission that pederasty is wrong—because youths must be abducted and not go willingly, yet it is accepted and even celebrated. Why resist what is good or innocent? Such resistance betrays some dim flicker of conscience that knows sex with boys is improper. Unfortunately, the reality of the sinful conscience is that it can be turned off altogether, and what is wrong can be justified as right and good.

Consideration of such practices may be unpleasant to Christian readers, but it serves to clarify the nature of the biblical witness. Our early Christian ancestors did not confess biblical chastity in a safe culture that naturally agreed with them. The sexual morality they taught and practiced stood out as unnatural to the Roman world just as Christian teachings about sex are labeled as unnatural in our day. The temptation many face today is to hide their confession for fear of how it will be received. They may believe that it is pointless to debate sexual morality in the public arena because the odds are stacked so hopelessly against them. But the social context of the early Christians shows that it is not hopeless.

---

[9] Strabo, *The Geography of Strabo*, vol. 5, trans. Horace Jones (London: William Heinemann Ltd. 1928), 155, 157.

The sexual climate in their day was worse in certain respects than it is today. Yet, they confessed Christ and stood firm in the sexual morality bound to His name.

To the Greeks and Romans, the love between a man and a boy was seen as superior to the love between a man and a woman. Lucian's (second century AD) *Affairs of the Heart* features a debate between two men, Lycinus and Callicratidas, over the topic of love. Lycinus makes the case that loving women is better than loving boys. Callicratidas favors the love of boys. Callicratidas argues,

> Let women be ciphers and be retained merely for child-bearing; but in all else away with them, and may I be rid of them. For what man of sense could endure from dawn onwards women who beautify themselves with artificial devices, women whose true form is unshapely, but who have extraneous adornments to beguile the unsightliness of nature? If at any rate one were to see women when they rise in the morning from last night's bed, one would think a woman uglier than those beasts whose name it is inauspicious to mention early in the day. That's why they closet themselves carefully at home and let no man see them.[10]

"Love" as it was described by Greek and Roman authors was the sexual engagement of equal minds. Plato and Socrates took this to the extent of resisting physical intercourse completely and focusing on intellectual engagement with other boys and men. There are stories of Socrates resisting the sexual advances of a young man and lying with him all night in embrace, never allowing their physical interaction to go beyond the embrace (much to the frustration of the young man who wanted it to go further). For most men, the physical sexual relationship was a natural extension of the meeting of equal minds. In Greek culture, sex for the sake of pure selfish physical gratification was socially denounced. They argued that intercourse with boys was a virtuous activity that benefited all of society.

---

[10] *Lucian*, Volume VIII, trans. by M. D. Macleod, Loeb Classical Library Volume 432 (Cambridge, MA: Harvard University Press, 1967), 210. Copyright © 1967 by the President and Fellows of Harvard College. Loeb Classical Library® is a registered trademark of the President and Fellows of Harvard College.

The gymnasium

This sexual exploitation of young boys began in the early adolescent years. Boys were trained to see themselves in bisexual terms. For example, a large element in the education of adolescent males was physical training through the local gymnasium. This was the place boys went to mold their bodies into the Roman male ideal. But their gyms were not like the gyms of today, where boys and girls play games in their gym uniforms. Activities in these ancient gyms were done in the nude. The word *gymnasium* comes from the Greek word γυμνός (*gymnos*) meaning "naked." The gymnasium is a Greek creation continued by the Romans, and one of the most popular activities for young boys at the gym was wrestling. Several ancient manuscripts have been found where wrestling coaches were accused of having intercourse with or fondling the boys during wrestling practice. Sexuality permeated Roman sports. The Olympic Games were initially run in the nude.

Certain scholars have argued that the gymnasium was frowned upon by Romans even as they continued the Greek practice. Some Romans thought the way boys were lavishly pampered with massages and body oiling contributed to a Greek softness that eventually led to the fall of Greece. Yet, these suspicions held by a number of Romans were not enough to eliminate the gymnasium. Throughout the Roman Empire, gyms flourished as focal points for adolescent boys. Girls were not permitted in the gym (except in ancient Sparta).

The very nature of these places put sexuality in the spotlight for boys. It required them not only to shed their clothes, but also their inhibitions and any sense of modesty. Indeed, modesty was not a Roman trait. The Roman gymnasium was a place that taught boys not to shun sexual interaction with other males. A geographer of the second century named Pausanias wrote a description of an athletic academy including a gymnasium just outside Athens. At the entrance to the academy was an altar dedicated to Eros, the god of erotic love.[11] Sex and athletics went together.

Knowing full well that the gymnasium would attract men given to pederasty, guidelines were established about who could and could not enter these gymnasiums and watch. Although local laws varied, in general, slaves were barred from entering the gymnasium as were all

---

[11] Hubbard, *Homosexuality in Greece and Rome*, 73. Quoting Pausanias 1.30.1.

women and young men between the ages of twenty and twenty four. (They were not yet considered mature enough to mentor a boy in a pederast relationship.) Others who met the criteria did frequent the gymnasium and did seduce boys into sexual relations, although, as previously noted, in the case of freeborn boys, a little more discretion was necessary.

Gymnasiums in the Roman Empire were said to be as common as hospitals in our day. Every reasonably sized town had one. They were a focal point of local activity and a magnet for sexual predation throughout the Roman Empire. Boys as young as twelve or thirteen began their physical training in the gymnasium and consequently began to be approached by adult men looking for intercourse. It had to be a terrifying time for young boys. There were a few Romans who objected to the sexual relationships between men and boys. They pointed out that such acts gave the boys nothing but tears and pain, and only the man was gratified. Yet despite some minor social resistance, the practice continued.

Christian sexual ethics that limited intercourse to the marriage of a man and a woman were not merely different from Roman ethics; they were utterly against Roman ideas of virtue and love. Roman perceptions of Christian sexual ideals would have been marked by hostility. Yet, Christians confessed what they believed to be true. As Christians today engage the world around them, they should not let hostility toward the biblical witness dissuade them. The first Christians were men and women of great courage. Confessing Christian morality always requires that spirit of bravery.

Womanhood and family

It should be fairly obvious to the reader that women were not always held in high regard in Roman society. Of course, there were exceptions to that rule. There are examples in ancient texts of virtuous wives being honored.[12] There was even a cult populated by wives who only had one husband. They worshipped the goddess of female virtue known as *pudicitia* (English trans. "modesty"). Yet there is a great deal of evidence

---

[12] Such as the story of Lucretia as told by Livy, whose virtue as a wife proved itself by her resisting the advances of another man only to be forced into intercourse. After having called her husband and having been cleared of wrongdoing, she committed suicide to preserve her honor. Cf. Rebecca Langlands, *Sexual Morality in Ancient Rome* (Cambridge: Cambridge University Press, 2006), 85–95.

that womanhood as a whole was not respected. Women were often seen as weak physically and mentally. They were inferior to men and existed to serve the men as little more than slaves at times.

In ancient Greece, married women were virtual prisoners in their homes. They were allowed to participate in certain religious rites and festivals but were not given social rites beyond that. It was expected that women, especially wealthy women, remain mostly confined to their homes.[13]

In Rome, women were given more rights. They were allowed to be educated up to a point. They could conduct trade and be seen in public, but they were denied a voice and vote in politics. One might be tempted to see this as an improvement of the status of women from the Greeks, and in some ways it is. But the overall opinion of Roman men toward women was abysmal by modern standards. This can be seen in more detail by looking at Roman practices in marriage.

The value of a Roman wife was often tied to her ability to have children. Women were usually married in their early teens and sometimes even at age 12. The average age of men getting married was slightly over twenty. The reason women tended to be married so young was to make the most of every year they could potentially bear children. The average life-span in the Roman Empire of Paul's day was about twenty five years.[14] The low average life-span must be seen in light of the extremely high mortality rates for children. It is believed that half of all children died before their sixth birthday.[15] This created a serious problem for the Roman Empire that sought to expand and grow throughout the known world. The population of Roman freeborn citizens did not keep pace with rates of expansion. Ideally, a married couple needed to have at least three children survive to adulthood for the population to grow. But with mortality rates at fifty percent for children under six and a life expectancy of only twenty five, a woman had to bear six or more children very quickly to do her part for population growth. Her value was tied to her ability to produce children quickly.

Once again we can see a contradiction in the Roman mind. While the ideal of a Roman male continuing his genetic line favored a woman hav-

---

[13] Michael Gagarin ed., *Oxford Encyclopedia of Ancient Greece and Rome*, vol. 3 (Oxford: Oxford University Press, 2010), 347.

[14] Arnold Lelis, William Percy, and Beert Verstraete, *The Age of Marriage in Ancient Rome* (New York: The Edwin Mellen Press, 2003), 24.

[15] Lelis, Percy, and Verstraete, *The Age of Marriage in Ancient Rome*, 24.

ing as many children as she could, many couples did not want multiple children. The wealthy in particular preferred to limit the number of their offspring. Infanticide was a common practice in Rome. The low rate of children being raised to maturity became so serious that Caesar Augustus passed a law known as the *lex Papia Poppaea* that granted rewards for those who had three or more children.[16] All these factors contributed to an overall view of womanhood that was largely negative. A woman's importance was rooted in her ability to have as many children as her husband wanted. Divorce on grounds of infertility seems to have been common. To understand how deeply ingrained this negative attitude toward women was, one needs only look at Greek and Roman explanations for the origin of women.

The primary creation story of woman accepted by the classical world came from Greek mythology. There, woman was created as a punishment for man. As the myth goes, the world was originally populated only by men. Zeus, angered by his brother Prometheus, who stole his fire and gave it to men, decided to get back at Prometheus by unleashing evil upon mankind. Zeus decided to create a new being that would vex mankind. He enlisted the help of the other gods. They each gave this new being special qualities, including great beauty and grace, to make her desirous and alluring to men. Her name was Pandora, which means "all gifts." She was endowed with all the gifts that men would find desirable. Unfortunately, she was also implanted with deceit, smooth words, and the habits of a thief. Pandora was given to a man named Epimetheus who immediately made her his wife. This man had been given a jar by the gods. It was filled with toils, diseases, and hardships. It also contained certain blessings. Prometheus gave Epimetheus strict orders never to open the jar. Pandora, driven by the evil planted within her by the gods, opened it despite her husband's instructions to the contrary. Immediately, the toils and pains that had been held back from humanity escaped from the jar and were let loose to vex men throughout the world. Hope, which was also in the jar, became caught under the lid and was not able to escape. Men have from then on trudged through life filled with pain and misery having only hope to give them strength.

The first written reference to Pandora comes from the Greek poet Hesiod (8th–7th century BC), who wrote, "From her is the race of

---

[16] J. A. Crook, *Law and Life of Rome 90 B.C.—A.D. 212* (Ithaca, NY: Cornell University Press, 1984), 46–47.

women and female kind: of her is the deadly race and tribe of women who live amongst mortal men to their great trouble, no helpmates in hateful poverty, but only in wealth, . . . *even so Zeus who thunders on high made women to be an evil to mortal men, with a nature to do evil.*"[17] In *Works and Days*, Hesiod again calls the woman "a plague to men who eat bread."[18] As Hesiod sees it, women were lechers who proved helpful only when their men could feed their insatiable appetite for wealth. Women existed to bring "great trouble" into the lives of men. The negative sentiments are by no means limited to Hesiod. Texts dating closer to the days of St. Paul are filled with complaints from men about the pains and sorrows brought on them by their wives.

At one lecture where I presented this, a woman sitting near the front asked me if I saw a connection between the Greek myth of Pandora and the biblical story of Eve. She felt that perhaps the Jews had borrowed from the Greek myth to create Eve. She pointed out that both Eve and Pandora were latecomers into a world where man already existed. Both were responsible for sin and misery—Eve by the eating of the forbidden fruit and Pandora by opening the jar. The point she was trying to make was that the Christian understanding of women was no better than the Greeks. Both seemed to blame woman for all the pain and misery in the world.

One has to agree that there is common ground in the stories up to a point. This common ground does not suggest the Jews stole the story from the Greeks or that both stories borrowed from a more ancient story. The biblical account of Eve by far predates that of Greek mythology. If anything, the Greeks borrowed ideas from Genesis and added their own negative opinions of women to the story, twisting it to create the myth of Pandora.

The dissimilarities between the stories reveal a radically different view of womanhood. Whereas Pandora was created as a punishment for man, Eve was created as a helper and companion to Adam. Eve completed Adam and filled the emptiness he had recognized in himself (Genesis 2:18, 20). Where Pandora is made separate from mankind, Eve was created out of the very flesh of Adam. She was not merely claimed by a man because he could not resist her (as was Pandora whose attributes

---

[17] Hesiod, "Theogony," 590–612, in *The Homeric Hymns and Homerica*, trans. Hugh G. Evelyn-White (New York: G. P. Putnam Sons, 1920), 123.

[18] Hesiod, "Works and Days," 80–85, in *The Homeric Hymns and Homerica*, 9.

were a trap), but was received by Adam with thanksgiving as a very part of him ("This is now bone of my bone and flesh of my flesh" [Genesis 2:23]). Pandora's "fall" is entirely the result of the designed weakness of womanhood. Zeus created her to hurt mankind. Eve's fall was the result of a failure in Adam who stood by and watched her sin without intervening. Thus, after the fall, God confronts Adam first and asks him, "Have you eaten of the tree that I commanded you not to eat?" (Genesis 3:11). Eve is not singled out as the sole source of sin in the biblical account as Pandora is in the Greek myth. Womanhood itself carries a positive understanding in Scripture.

Negative views about women in Roman society drove an additional wedge between Roman and Christian ideals. "Misogyny" became an excuse for Roman men to be unfaithful to their wives. While verbally affirming marital fidelity in marriage rites, the unspoken rule in Roman society was that men would have other lovers. Many times those lovers were boys. Martial (AD 40–104), a Spanish poet who wrote in Rome several decades after St. Paul, chastises women for being jealous when their husbands had intercourse with slave boys. He tells the wife to be thankful that she is the only woman in her husband's life, and further to accept the fact that she cannot offer the same level of quality sex that slave boys can.[19] One finds other writers telling wives not to worry about their husbands showing affection to boys because boys will grow up and cease to be attractive to men, at which time the wife will be the center of her husband's attention again.

A married woman was considered to be under the authority of her husband. He had legal rights over her. Unlike the biblical model, she did not have those same rights over him. He was legally free to exercise his male sexual desires with others outside the marriage. If he committed adultery with a woman of high social standing, he might find himself in legal trouble because his sexual partner was under the authority of a man with legal means.[20] Yet if he committed adultery with slaves or prostitutes or if he had a concubine, there was no legal recourse for the wife. It was a different matter, though, if a woman cheated on her husband. A woman caught with another male (man or boy) could be charged as an adulteress. Her male partner was also guilty under law. Cato the Younger (95–46 BC), who was concerned with immorality in Rome, complained

---

[19] Williams, *Roman Homosexuality*, 50.
[20] Crook, *Law and Life of Rome 90 B.C.—A.D. 212*, 101.

about the double standard in marriage.[21] The legal penalty for adultery allowed the husband to rape the male offender and then, if he desired, to kill his wife. Prior to Caesar Augustus, a husband was allowed to forgive his wife's infidelities. Augustus, however, made it illegal for a husband to pardon his wife for sex crimes. He was legally obligated—at a minimum—to divorce his wife if she was caught in adultery.[22] It is not enough to suggest that women were under-appreciated in Roman culture. There are many instances where they were treated as second-class human beings, slightly more honored than slaves.

As will be shown in the following chapters, St. Paul's treatment of women accords them a status of honor unheard of in Roman culture. This greater appreciation for womanhood is a necessary element in Paul's overall view of sexuality. It would have made the Christian position all the more radical and counter-cultural. In Christendom, a woman found a culture of genuine love that saw her as equally important as any man in the eyes of God. She was sexually equal with the man in the marriage union and had equal recourse under the law of God to demand marital fidelity. To the Romans, Paul's views would have been seen as disruptive to the social fabric and demeaning of the Roman ideal of masculinity.

a World of promiscuity

In many ways, ancient Roman culture represents the kind of sexual utopia many long for today. There were very few sexual boundaries in comparison with today's moral standards. Monogamy was rarely practiced. The Stoic philosophers were among the few voices that spoke in favor of monogamy in marriage. Sadly, we seem to be approaching the same level of hedonism in our world today. Sexual activity and intercourse before marriage have become a cultural expectation. Young couples who refrain from intercourse until they are married are in a small minority. Statistics from a 2011 Centers for Disease Control study claim that about half of all high school students admit to having intercourse (though slightly more males than females).[23] By the time they graduate high school, the same CDC study says that 63% of young adults admit to

---

[21] Williams, *Roman Homosexuality*, 51.

[22] Crook, *Law and Life of Rome 90 B.C.—A.D. 212*, 106.

[23] Centers for Disease Control and Prevention, "Sexual Risk Behavior: HIV, STD, & Teen Pregnancy Prevention," www.cdc.gov/HealthyYouth/sexualbehaviors/ (accessed February 3, 2016).

having intercourse. As people get older, monogamy becomes harder to find. The CDC reports that statistics from 2011–2013 show men between the ages of twenty-five to forty-four have on average 6.6 sexual partners, while women of the same age group claim an average of 4.3 partners.[24]

The difference between Rome in the days of the apostles and Western civilization today has more to do with social acceptance than the kinds of sins committed. Promiscuity in ancient Rome was much more in the open and enjoyed general public acceptance. Homosexual acts among men were accepted socially. Married men were expected to have trysts. Rape of slaves was a given. In short, the Roman ideal of the conquering male allowed him to exercise a level of sexual exploitation that today would be considered socially unacceptable. That being said, social acceptance is an ever changing thing and what is not acceptable today might be in the future.

The example of rome's leaders

The clearest picture of how open and sanctioned immoral behavior was in Roman culture can be seen in the lives of the Caesars. A country's leaders tend to reflect the moods and attitudes of prevailing culture and set the tone for society. Leaders are both watched and emulated. At this point in our American history, one can see public figures falling all over themselves to make statements that support homosexuality because the public trend is toward the acceptance of it. They wish to identify with the perceived majority to secure favor with the masses and thus ensure their future election. That is how politics work. In emulating culture, they also further those agendas that they emulate. More people jump on the bandwagon because the officials they like have shown support for this or that cause. The same dynamic was at work in Rome.

A culture of promiscuity produced leaders who were promiscuous, which furthered the agenda of sexual immorality, which led to leaders who were even more immoral. It was a vicious circle. As will be shown below, the sexual immorality of Rome was part of a much greater objectification of human beings. A review of some of the key leaders of Rome during the time of Christ and apostles shows not only a pattern of

---

[24] Centers for Disease Control and Prevention, "Key Statistics from the National Survey of Family Growth," www.cdc.gov/nchs/nsfg/key_statistics/n.htm#numberlifetime (accessed February 3, 2016).

sexual promiscuity among Roman leaders but an utter disregard for life and the dignity of others. The Caesars reflected the mind of the people, and the people reflected the mind of the Caesars.

The Roman biographer Suetonius (AD 69–122) wrote about the lives of the first twelve Caesars. Modern scholarship has pointed out that some of the stories he relates about the Caesars may be anecdotal—meaning that some of them may be exaggerated stories that were floating around in public conversation. Others, however, believe that much of what he wrote is factual. Whether all of what he wrote is one-hundred percent accurate or not is beside the point; what matters is that his writings reflect the public perception of these men that was influencing society at the time. The stories of their sexual exploits shaped culture as well as reflected it.

CAESAR AUGUSTUS (31 BC–AD 14)

Caesar Augustus was the leader of Rome when Jesus was born. Augustus is often portrayed as one of the most fair-minded and level-headed of all the Caesars. His rule, which lasted forty years, was looked upon as a model for others to emulate. Yet, Augustus's sexual exploits were well-known by the general public.

> Sextus Pompey reproached him with being an effeminate fellow; and M. Antony, with earning his adoption from his uncle by prostitution. Lucius Antony, likewise Mark's brother, charges him with pollution by Caesar; and that, for a gratification of three hundred thousand sesterces, he had submitted to Aulus Hirtius in the same way, in Spain; adding, that he used to singe his legs with burnt nutshells, to make the hair become softer.[25]

There were stories of Augustus inviting senators to dinner, then taking the wife of a senator from the table to his bedroom only to return her with her hair in a mess and her ears glowing red. Suetonius tells of how in his later years, Augustus's wife help him find beautiful young virgins from throughout the empire, who were taken to him to "deflower."[26]

---

[25] Suetonius, *Lives of the Twelve Caesars*, 121.

[26] Suetonius, *Lives of the Twelve Caesars*, 124.

TIBERIUS (AD 14-37)

Following the death of Augustus, Tiberius reigned. His sexual immorality exceeded Augustus. He is said to have created a new publicly funded office for attending to his sexual pleasures.[27] His retreat on the isle of Capri was created to be a sexual playground for his fantasies.

> In his retreat at Capri, he also contrived an apartment containing couches, and adapted to the secret practice of abominable lewdness, where he entertained companies of girls and catamites, and assembled from all quarters inventors of unnatural copulations, whom he called *Spintriae*, who defiled one another in his presence, to inflame by the exhibition the languid appetite. . . . He likewise contrived recesses in woods and groves for the gratification of lust, where young persons of both sexes prostituted themselves in caves and hollow rocks, in the disguise of little Pans and Nymphs.[28]

Tiberius was known to practice pedophilia. He found pretty boys and trained them to swim with him in his pool in perverse ways. They were to swim between his thighs and "nibble on his private parts." Tacitus supports Suetonius's claims about the Emperor, recording that Tiberius debauched freeborn children and was guilty of sexual abominations so perverse that new names had to be invented for them.[29] Such unspeakable behavior was not prosecuted. Tiberius was a sexual predator, a rapist, pedophile, and bi-sexual adulterer. He does not seem to have been well-liked by the public. A neighboring king wrote him accusing him of murder, cowardice, and sexual perversity and suggested he kill himself to satisfy the hatred of his own people.[30] Yet Tiberius's deeds stood without public trial and punishment. This was the Roman Emperor in power when Christ was crucified. When the Jews shouted at Jesus' trial that they had no king but Caesar (John 19:15), this was the Caesar whom they were willing to serve. Jesus was a greater offense to them than Tiberius.

---

[27] Suetonius, *Lives of the Twelve Caesars*, 219.

[28] Suetonius, *Lives of the Twelve Caesars*, 219.

[29] Tacitus, *The Annals, Books IV–VI, XI–XII*, trans. John Jackson (Cambridge, MA: Harvard University Press, 1998), 155.

[30] Suetonius, *Lives of the Twelve Caesars*, 233.

CALIGULA (AD 37-41)

If one were to take a psychopathic serial killer and give him absolute power, one would end up with something like Caligula. Though it was never proven, credible rumors circulated that Caligula was complicit in the death of Tiberius. Publicly, Tiberius was said to die of natural causes, but Caligula was suspected of poisoning him. Caligula was the adopted grandson of Tiberius.

Since the days of Julius, the Caesars were considered divine. Caligula, however, took his divine status to new heights. He ordered all the images of the gods that were famous to be brought from Greece. He then commanded that their heads be removed and carved images of his own head be put on them. Caligula actually had a temple constructed in his own honor, instituted a priesthood to serve there, had a golden idol of himself cast, and developed a sacrificial system devoted to his worship.[31] His golden idol was dressed daily in such a way as to reflect the clothes he normally wore.

Caligula commanded the murder of his brother and forced his father-in-law to commit suicide. He lived incestuously with his sisters. He took one of his sisters, named Drusilla, from her husband and openly lived with her as his wife until her death by an illness. Sex and marriage meant nothing to Caligula. It is reported that he went to a wedding as a guest and had the bride seized and taken to his home where he married her and then came to hate her shortly thereafter.[32]

There are several stories of Caligula inviting married couples to dinner. If one of the wives caught his fancy, he would take her into an adjoining room, rape her, and then come back to dinner and talk openly to his guests about her qualities as a lover. His passions included homosexual acts as well. Caligula reportedly had sex with male actors, freedmen, and hostages. Suetonius relates that Caligula enjoyed cross-dressing.[33]

The most notable aspect of this Caesar was his utter disregard for human life and his cruel inhumanity toward all people. He would order the execution of people brought before him for trial without even hearing

---

[31] Dio Cassius, *Roman History*, Volume VII: Books 56–60, trans. by Earnest Cary on the basis of the version of Herbert Baldwin Foster, Loeb Classical Library Volume 175 (Cambridge MA: Harvard University Press, 1924), 353, 355. Loeb Classical Library® is a registered trademark of the President and Fellows of Harvard College.

[32] Cassius, *Roman History*, Volume VII, 267.

[33] Suetonius, *Lives of the Twelve Caesars*, 286–287.

their cases. He had people tortured and murdered as dinner entertainment. On one occasion, he brought in a soldier skilled at beheading for the purposes of entertaining him. He would force parents to watch the execution of their children and would then joke with them afterward. He had a playwright burned alive in the arena for writing verses with double meanings, and he had a senator murdered, torn apart, and his limbs and guts piled in a heap before him.[34] Cassius records an incident where there were not enough condemned criminals to throw to wild beasts in the arena, so he ordered that some of the spectators be thrown to the beasts. To prevent them from protesting against him, he had their tongues cut out.[35] There are many stories of murder and gross cruelty committed by Caligula. He ruled Rome for less than four years, from AD 37–41. Yet, it should be noted that these were critical years for Christianity. It was in his empire that the Christian Gospel started to spread. His vicious cruelty stood in contrast to the self-sacrificing love of Christ that was being proclaimed by the apostles.

CLAUDIUS (AD 41-54)

Claudius became Caesar following Caligula. Of all the Caesars described by Suetonius, Claudius is the only one reported to have an aversion to homosexual activity. He supposedly did not care for homosexual sex and preferred women. His heterosexual sins, however, were certainly consistent with the mindset of the age. He was married six times, one of which was to his niece and thus an incestuous relationship. Suetonius claims that there were no bounds to his lust for women.[36]

Claudius holds the distinction of being the first Caesar to officially react against Christians. Suetonius states that he "banished from Rome all the Jews, who were continually making disturbances at the instigation of one Chrestus."[37] We are not told what those "disturbances" were, but in all likelihood it was the Christian refusal to participate in the idolatry and immorality of prevailing culture. This shows us how within only a decade of Jesus' death and resurrection, the Christian Gospel had reached Rome and was causing disturbances at the highest levels. God sent word of His grace and forgiveness into a place like Rome that was utterly hostile to

---

[34] Suetonius, *Lives of the Twelve Caesars*, 271–272.

[35] Cassius, *Roman History*, Volume VII, 291.

[36] Suetonius, *Lives of the Twelve Caesars*, 324.

[37] Suetonius, *Lives of the Twelve Caesars*, 318. Cf. Acts 18:2.

Christian morality and ethics. It was a Gospel carried by Jewish converts who were anxious to share their newfound hope with the Gentiles around them and who consequently were punished for it.

The objectification of human beings (that is, treating them as mere objects to be used) continued under Claudius, though not to the extent of Caligula. His cruelty is exemplified by stories of punishing criminals, especially those who were guilty of parricide, by flogging them, sewing them in a sack with wild animals, and throwing them into the sea.[38] He enjoyed watching prisoners executed and ordered gladiators butchered before him so he could see their faces as they took their last gasps of breath.[39] Some of his cruelty was of his own initiative. At other times, the weakness of his character simply went along with the bloodlust of others.[40]

NERO (AD 54-68)

Nero is an especially important figure for Christians. Tradition has it that both St. Paul and St. Peter were killed in Rome under the authority of Nero. When a terrible fire consumed Rome, Nero placed blame for it on Christians and thus made Christianity greatly hated throughout the empire. Nero's own cruelty against Christians is legendary. The Roman historian Tacitus records that Nero would tie Christians to stakes and set them on fire to light his garden at night. Christians were sewn into animal skins and thrown into the arena to be ripped apart by dogs.[41]

From Nero's day, claims were leveled against Christians charging them with atheism, immorality, and rejection of the Roman way of life. It was because Christians would only worship the one true triune God and would not participate in the public worship of Rome's traditional gods that they were accused of atheism. Christians refused to acknowledge the deity of the Caesars, which made them enemies of Rome's rulers and thus of Rome itself. Christian morality rejected the wanton sexual exploitation of human beings that defined so much of Rome's sexual culture, and for this, they were accused of immorality. Because Christians claimed their

---

[38] Thomas DeCoursey Ruth, "The Problem of Claudius" (PhD diss. John Hopkins University, 1916), 86.

[39] Suetonius, *Lives of the Twelve Caesars*, 324.

[40] Cassius, *Roman History*, Volume VII, 401.

[41] Cornelius Tacitus, *Annals of Tacitus*, trans. Alfred Church and William Brodribb (New York: The MacMillan Co., 1921), 305.

citizenship was in heaven, they were accused of rejecting the common good of other Roman citizens. Christianity was seen as a radical and hated religion.

As the Gospel was brought into the Jewish communities living in these Roman towns, the Jews were at times resistant. Many did not accept the teaching that Christ was the Messiah for whom Judaism had been waiting. Hostile Jews sought out Roman civil leaders and secured Roman force for eliminating Christian missionaries. Acts 17 describes how the Jewish community in Thessalonica rose up against Paul and Silas (vv. 1–9). When they could not find the disciples, they attacked the man at whose home Paul and Silas were staying. They dragged him in front of the Roman authorities and accused the Christians of sedition against the Roman government. "These men who have turned the world upside down have come here also, and Jason has received them, and they are all acting against the decrees of Caesar, saying that there is another king, Jesus" (vv. 6–7). The message of Christ with its unyielding devotion to the one true God, rejection of all other gods, focus on Christ as the sole Savior of humanity, and its insistence on moral chastity was "turning the world upside down." The Jews found an ally with Rome against the Christian message.

Nero helped incite the Romans against Christians. He indulged Roman hatred by singling out Christians for special tortures. As Suetonius described it, "He likewise inflicted punishments on the Christians, a sort of people who held a new and impious superstition."[42] Nero's immorality would have set him against the Christian message. He had an incestuous relationship with his mother, whom he later had murdered. He is the first Caesar to have been married to another man in a public ceremony (more on this in the next section). He was complicit in his father's death and murdered his brothers and his wife. Like Caligula, Nero enjoyed cross-dressing in public on occasion. Rape was a game for Nero. He is known to have had children tied to stakes, and then, wearing an animal hide to terrorize them, he would sexually assault them, pretending to eat parts of their bodies.[43]

---

[42] Suetonius, *Lives of the Twelve Caesars*, 347.

[43] Dio Cassius, *Roman History,* Volume VIII: Books 61–70, trans. by Earnest Cary on the basis of the version of Herbert Baldwin Foster, Loeb Classical Library Volume 176 (Cambridge, MA: Harvard University Press, 1925), 159. Loeb Classical Library® is a registered trademark of the President and Fellows of Harvard College.

Knowing what the Caesars were like and how hostile they were to Christians makes Paul's appeal to Caesar all the more shocking. Acts 25:7–12 tells of St. Paul being judged before Festus. His accusers were Jews who rejected his message. Festus gave Paul the choice to be judged in Jerusalem by the Jews or in Rome by Caesar. Paul appealed to Caesar. As a Roman citizen, he had the right to have his case heard by Caesar. But Paul, being a Roman citizen and knowing the nature of the Caesars, would have known his case had no chance. He was signing his own death warrant. What his appeal to Caesar would accomplish was to buy him time and a broader Gentile audience for the proclamation of the Gospel.

The Roman Caesars described above were living icons of immorality and cruelty. Sex was used as a means of domination and self-gratification. Their sexual immorality was linked to severe cruelty to other people. They were the supreme Roman males who took what they wanted when and how they wanted it, regardless of who they had to hurt to get it. Christian morality, which taught the sacrifice of the self for others, was utterly alien to the Caesars' worldview.

Reviewing the terrible deeds of the Caesars from the years when the Christian Church was in its infancy offers encouragement for the Christian witness today. Publicly defining sexual morality in terms contrary to the practice of the Caesars did not just threaten the early Christians with unpopularity, it put them at risk of death. A mere commitment to traditions cannot explain their willingness to put their lives on the line. Only an unwavering belief that God's ways are superior to those of the establishment, and that even in death God's grace would bring them life, can explain their boldness. Christians in America today may fear negative reactions as they stand by God's Word and call the practices of the world to account, but in truth, the first Christians had much more to fear. Yet, through the radically different morality Christians exemplified, God successfully called individuals away from the hedonism glorified in Roman culture. It is strong evidence that engagement with the world is not pointless even when sexual immorality seems to control society.

It is difficult for modern readers to appreciate the nature of the risk Christians faced by challenging the morality of the Caesars. To challenge the morality of Caesar was tantamount to mocking god, and mocking the universal god of Rome was to attack the heart of Roman society. Worship of the Caesars (a.k.a. the "imperial cult") was a mark of being a Roman and considered essential for the strength of the nation. In his book *Roman Society*, Henry Boren writes:

> The provincial councils, made up of upper-class men, gave much attention to the imperial cult; so also did the augustales, priestly colleges of freedmen. Other priestly colleges included rites to the emperors in their regular observances: and the army too made much of the cult, for example, in oaths and through observing birth dates. The imperial cult thus touches the lives of persons in all social strata. The proper observance of its ceremonies became a symbol of patriotism as well as of piety.[44]

Patriotism and Caesar-worship went hand in hand. To be opposed to the worship of Caesar was to be opposed to Rome itself.

Similar things happen in American society. To challenge prevailing morality, especially if it is espoused by a charismatic leader, is seen as an attack on America itself. America, so the argument goes, is built on pluralism and diversity of every sort. These, in turn, are showcased by the politically elite. An example of this was seen at a recent visit by the pope to the White House; the president placed people on the guest list who were known opponents of Roman Catholic doctrine on sexual morality. Their presence was understood by many Catholics as a not-so-subtle message that sexual diversity is positive and Catholic doctrine needs to change.[45] Moral plurality has become a mark of patriotism. To insist that Christian sexual morality is better or more God-pleasing than other views is seen as an attack on the very fabric of our culture. Fortunately, the penalties we face for disagreeing with the status quo are still nothing compared to the cost of faithfulness for the first Christians.

Christians of every age do have an important advantage over a sexually hedonistic and permissive culture: compassion. As Rome demonstrated, a product of sexual hedonism is the objectification of human beings. The lust of the Caesars left a trail of death, destruction, and broken lives. Christians answered this cruelty with love and care for

---

[44] Henry C. Boren, *Roman Society*, 2nd ed. (Lexington, MA: D. C. Heath and Co., 1992), 291.

[45] Kevin B. Jones, "What's Behind the White House's Invite to Catholic Dissenters," Catholic News Agency, September 18, 2015, www.catholicnewsagency.com/news/whats-behind-the-white-houses-invite-to-catholic-dissenters-13715/ (accessed February 3, 2016).

others, even for their enemies. They placed sex within the context of committed bonds of marital love. They denounced sex as a means to satisfy one's own selfish desires. When a broader compassion for humanity is joined to biblical sexual morality, it is much more difficult to label Christians as unloving. During one of my lectures, a young woman asked if I would ever help someone whom I knew was homosexual. She wanted to see if a message of sexual fidelity went hand in hand with compassion. Not only would I help someone whom I knew was homosexual, I had recently done so and was able to share the example with her. There are many in our society, as there were in Roman society, who have been victimized by sexual hedonism. Genuine concern for them, joined with a message of sexual chastity, can point them to the Savior whose love stands ready to forgive and restore those broken by sin.

other expressions of sexual promiscuity

PROSTITUTION

We have noted above that prostitution was legal in the Roman Empire. Taxes on prostitutes contributed significant amounts to local treasuries. In Corinth, where St. Paul ministered to a small congregation, the temple of Aphrodite was a prominent feature. When Corinth was under Greek control, the temple there is rumored to have had more than a thousand prostitutes at work, making Corinth a hub for sex tourism. An Olympic athlete named Xenophon of Corinth once donated a hundred young girls as prostitutes to this temple as a gift of thanksgiving to Aphrodite after having won the Pentathlon. The sexual promiscuity of Corinth was legendary in the ancient world. Aristophanes coined the term *korinthiazomai*, meaning "I act like a Corinthian," in reference to sexual immorality.[46] Plato described women given to prostitution as "Corinthian girls" in "The Republic."[47]

In 146 BC, Corinth was destroyed as punishment for its role in a revolt against Rome. It was rebuilt by Julius Caesar in 44 BC. By Paul's day, the temple to Aphrodite was considerably smaller than in its heyday, and it was under Roman control, but the culture of promiscuity

---

[46] Simon Hornblower, *The Greek World 479–323 B.C.* 4th ed. (New York, NY: Routledge, 2011), 119.

[47] Plato, *The Dialogues of Plato*, vol. 3, *The Republic*, bk. 3, trans. B. Jowett (New York: Oxford University Press, 1892), 91.

remained. It was in Corinth where Paul had to address a case of incest among the newly converted Christians (1 Corinthians 5:1).

Prostitution was tied to the worship of certain Roman deities. There is some debate about the extent of temple prostitution in the Roman Empire, and it does seem that it was more prevalent in earlier Greek culture than in the Rome of St. Paul's day. But there were certain deities among the Romans understood as fertility gods (or goddesses) where temple prostitution was practiced. Aphrodite (Greek), also known as Venus, was one such goddess who was worshipped through ritualistic sex. Most scholars seem to agree that Diana was worshipped through ritualistic sex, though others contend that she was not. Even one of St. Paul's companions, Silas (Silvanus), who was a Gentile convert, was named after a Greek god worshipped through ritualistic sex.

One of the later Roman emperors, Elagabalus (AD 203–222) actually enjoyed playing the part of a prostitute. He would go to brothels and compete with the women for male lovers. He went so far as to turn the royal palace into a brothel, where he would stand naked in the door and offer himself to passing men.[48] Prostitution was yet another dimension of objectifying human beings and separating sexual intercourse from love or compassion. Jesus raised the suspicion of the religious leadership of His day because of His association with prostitutes (Luke 7:36–50). The woman called "a sinner" by the Pharisee in Luke 7 was obviously ashamed of her life of sexual promiscuity, but she came to Jesus seeking mercy. Without any public censure for her immoral life, Jesus announced God's forgiveness to her. He did not treat her as an object, but a person precious to the heavenly Father. That compassion, which was so willing to forgive, coupled with a message of a sexually purer life in Christ, drew those who were broken by sexual immorality to the Christian Church.

SAME-SEX MARRIAGE

The public debate over same-sex marriage is one that many Christians wish they could avoid. Parishioners tell me how hesitant they are to discuss the topic with friends and family because of the explosive reactions they have received when it has come up in the past. Same-sex

---

[48] Dio Cassius, *Roman History*, Volume IX: Books 71–80, trans. by Earnest Cary on the basis of the version of Herbert Baldwin Foster, Loeb Classical Library Volume 177 (Cambridge, MA: Harvard University Press, 1927), 463. Loeb Classical Library® is a registered trademark of the President and Fellows of Harvard College.

marriage was legalized in the state of Iowa, where I live, in 2009. It was the third state in the country to do so. Now, only six years later, same-sex marriage has been legalized throughout the country through the decree of the Supreme Court. Every year, public opinion becomes more accepting of same-sex marriage. Those who push the homosexual agenda claim that it is a sign of progress. It is presented as if it is something new and beneficial for society. Those who stand against same-sex marriage are painted as repressive traditionalists who fight against progress, or worse, as criminals who violate civil rights.

In point of fact, same-sex marriage in not a new phenomenon. Though it was not a common practice in St. Paul's day, the Roman sexual climate did allow for it. Late in his reign, which ended in AD 68, Nero was not only married to one man, but two.

> Now Nero called Sporus "Sabina" not merely because, owing to his resemblance to her he had been made a eunuch, but because the boy, like the mistress, had been solemnly married to him in Greece, Tigellinus giving the bride away, as the law ordained. All the Greeks held a celebration in honour of their marriage, uttering all the customary good wishes, even to the extent of praying that legitimate children might be born to them. After that Nero had two bedfellows at once, Pythagoras to play the role of husband to him, and Sporus that of wife. The latter, in addition to other forms of address, was termed "lady," "queen," and "mistress."[49]

According to the description of Dio Cassius, Sporus was a transvestite. He dressed as a woman and presented himself as a woman. He was castrated to arrest his sexual development. His function in the relationship was to play the wife sexually. Cassius shows that this marriage was apparently accepted and even celebrated by members of the community. Nero regularly went out to public events with Sporus as his wife. Undoubtedly, not everyone would have looked upon this favorably, but it does seem clear that by and large the Roman community accepted it.

About 150 years later, Elagabalus (a.k.a. Marcus Aurelius Antoninus Augustus, AD 203–222) followed Nero's example and was married to a man. His "husband" was a Carian slave named Hierocles. Elagabalus is described by Dio Cassius as sometimes wearing eye makeup and a hair-

---

[49] Dio Cassius, *Roman History*, Volume VIII, 159.

net. He is said to have shaved his face smooth to appear as a woman.[50] As noted previously, homosexual intercourse did not call into question one's "manhood" in the Roman mind, provided the man in question was the one doing the sodomizing and not receiving it. Elagabalus broke with tradition and openly played the female in the sexual relationship.

Elagabalus is also known to have had at least three female wives and still more women lovers all by the age of eighteen. Dio Cassius records that Elagabalus went so far as to order his physicians surgically to create an incision in his body that could function as a female vagina for homoerotic intercourse.[51] The physicians evidently did not comply.

The extreme examples of Nero and Elagabalus were not the norm for Roman society. But there can be no question that leaders do both reflect prevailing attitudes and set the tone for the rest of society. Rome's leaders set a tone of sexual permissiveness and self-gratification that created an atmosphere of extreme hostility toward Christian notions of sexual chastity and self-emptying love. Social hostility did not dissuade the early Christians from making their case for sexual morality; it should not frustrate the Christian message in our day either.

rome's self-image and the vestal virgins

It is a curious aspect of human nature that it cannot see itself as it really is. Paul comments on this to the Corinthians: "If we judged ourselves truly, we would not be judged" (1 Corinthians 11:31). We as sinful beings are incapable of rightly judging ourselves because we are incapable of seeing the true nature of our own failings before God. We judge ourselves from what God's Word tells us about our heart and mind, not on the basis of how we feel about ourselves. Where the Word of God is absent, so, too, is a person's ability to see him or herself rightly.

This was certainly the case in Rome. Despite the sexually promiscuous practices documented above, there is evidence that the image Rome had of itself was an image of chastity and honor. One Roman scholar has even suggested that the Romans were more concerned with morality than any other ancient people.[52] This he bases on the various Roman virtues taught by the many mythological stories that permeated Roman culture.

---

[50] Cassius, *Roman History,* Volume IX, 465.

[51] Cassius, *Roman History,* Volume IX, 471.

[52] Michael Grant, *Roman Myths* (New York: Charles Scribner's Sons, 1971), 224.

Indeed, the myths do teach certain virtues like courage, strength, cunning, devotion to others, patriotism, and sacrifice, to name a few. Religion and myth were in service to the state, and those qualities of each that proved useful to the state were lauded. The image Rome wanted to project of itself was an image of virtue. The prominence of the Vestal Virgins in Rome represents a public attempt to portray Rome in terms of sexual purity. Author Ariadne Staples makes the case in her book *From Good Goddess to Vestal Virgins* that Vestal Virgins were living representations of Rome as a whole.[53]

Vestal Virgins were chosen by strict criteria from Roman girls, free of all physical defects or blemishes, between the ages of six and ten, raised in sound homes by Roman parents. The terms of their service as Vestal Virgins lasted for thirty years. There were usually six Vestal Virgins serving simultaneously. At the end of thirty years, they could leave their office and be married. Their term of service coincided with the period of life wherein women would be most sexually active and most likely to bear children.

When the Vestal Virgin appeared in public, she was always accompanied by an officer. This officer was a symbol of Roman power. Only certain high officials would be so accompanied. Anyone seeing a woman accompanied by such an officer would immediately know this was a Vestal Virgin. She was free to attend the same public and private gatherings afforded to any Roman woman but was expected in dress and conduct to present herself modestly. It was this outward modesty that was to be the public symbol of Rome's collective integrity.[54]

One of the main duties of Vestal Virgins was to tend the hearth fire in the temple of Vesta. Any Roman could draw a flame from the hearth fire to start a fire in his or her home. The Vestal then symbolically served as house mother to every Roman home. The Vestals were also mother figures to the Roman ideal. According to Roman mythology, Romulus, the father of Rome, and Remus, his twin brother, were said to be born of a Vestal Virgin named Rhea Silvia. There are various stories of how she became pregnant, but one of the most prominent is that she was impregnated by the god Mars, who either raped her with her knowledge or while she slept. The Vestal Virgins were Rome's image of itself and its founda-

---

[53] Ariadne Staples, *From Good Goddess to Vestal Virgins: Sex and Category in Roman Religion* (London and New York: Routledge, 1998), 147.

[54] Staples, *From Good Goddess to Vestal Virgins*, 147.

tion. They were mother to Rome and yet chaste and virginal. Their influence touched every god or goddess to whom sacrifices were offered. Every sacrifice to any of the gods of Rome was sprinkled with special salted flour called *mola salsa* made exclusively by the Vestal Virgins.[55]

The grotesque irony that Rome made such efforts publicly to identify itself with a symbol of civilized morality and virtue when the social fabric was so interwoven with pagan hedonism is shocking, but such is the nature of unbelief. The old adage that people see what they want to see is true. Unless the Holy Spirit opens the mind to understand its situation, the mind remains dark and unable to see itself rightly. The damage done to individual lives and to society as a whole by sexual immorality seems obvious to Christians. But it is not obvious to those who are immersed in it. In fact, many of those who champion acceptance of diverse sexual expressions believe that sex without love, fidelity, or lifelong marital commitment is a virtue.

How, then, can Christians debate those who do not see the negative effects of sexual hedonism, who may even see promiscuity as an advantageous quality? Debate itself will not convince anyone whose mind is willingly closed. Instead of looking to win arguments, Christians should approach discussions with the goal of planting seeds that the Holy Spirit may or may not bring to fruit. Pointing to Christ's forgiveness for sexual sins, speaking of repentance, and talking about the benefits of sexual fidelity and genuine love for others as a product of Christ's grace is enough. The majority will remain hardened against Christ; they will shut out the Christian message. But there will be individuals whom the Holy Spirit reaches. Legends suggest that more than one Vestal converted to Christianity: Daria who was executed in AD 283, was a Vestal who encouraged others to follow Christ; and Coelia Concordia, who was said to be the last chief Vestal, converted to Christianity around AD 400.

Summary

The Christian converts to whom Paul ministered had been influenced their whole lives by very open sexually promiscuous behavior, pornographic art, sexually suggestive theater, and religious rituals that sometimes included sex acts. Paul brought Christ to people who had themselves been sexually exploited. I have no doubt that in some of the

---

[55] Staples, *From Good Goddess to Vestal Virgins*, 154.

congregations he founded there would have been male members who had homosexual experiences, made use of prostitutes, and even participated in the sexual abuse of slaves. Men who committed such things were not uncommon in that culture.

Claims in our day of being progressive and moving forward by accepting the "new" prevailing views on sexuality and same-sex marriage are horribly misinformed. Acceptance of homosexuality and same-sex marriage is nothing new at all. It is not "progressive;" it is "regressive." Contemporary views about sexuality are simply a revival of an older and much less loving view of the world. Open sexual practices do not set people free to love more. The example of Rome bears out that sexual hedonism serves only to objectify human beings and thereby erode social peace.

Though Christian morality promoted genuine self-emptying love and was positive for society, it nonetheless set Christ's people against the prevailing culture. Romans did not like being told that some of their favorite activities were displeasing to the Christian God, and they pushed back. Still today, proponents of sexual immorality are not content to practice their ways behind closed doors; they demand public approval. In the first century, when Christians refused to approve, they became enemies of humanity itself in the Roman mind.

Secular society is moving ever closer to Rome in its assessment of Christianity. The message of Christ is despised, and Christians are seen as bigoted and unloving. Christians today can learn from the Christians who lived in the Roman Empire of St. Paul's day. The bubble of social acceptance for Christian morality has burst, and now we must be prepared to suffer. Those who speak God's truth in love will be hated. They may even be prosecuted in some instances. What the example of Rome shows us is that despite the best efforts of the world to silence the message of Christ, His truth will continue. The more Rome persecuted Christians, the more the Holy Spirit worked to bring faith and life in Christ to the lost.

chapter 2

THE JEWISH CONTEXT

From the previous chapter, it should be evident that Paul was certainly not trying to conserve an ethical view in keeping with traditional Roman morality. In Rome, traditional conservative morality would have favored bisexual activity, rape of non-Roman citizens, and repression of women. The way Paul presented sexual morality in his epistles was a radical departure from Roman morality. Nor is it fair to say that Paul was bringing a conservative Jewish morality to the sexual practices of Rome. Paul's teachings represent a departure from what would have been considered traditional Jewish views about sex.

When seeking to define those traditional Jewish views, sources are difficult to find. Naturally the Jews looked to the Old Testament to define their ethics of sexuality. The Old Testament is the clearest Jewish authority and the only written ethical code followed by the Jews in Paul's day. However, there was also a strong oral tradition of laws among the rabbis of Paul's day that defined sexual conduct and practice. This oral tradition presented differing interpretations of Old Testament law. In the first century, the two main competing schools of oral tradition were the house of Hillel and the house of Shammai. These "houses" represented groups of rabbis who studied the Torah (first five books of the Old Testament) and rendered opinions. The weakness of oral law rested in the minds of those who transmitted it. It was wholly dependent on memory to transmit complex arguments. To solve the problem, a rabbi named Judah HaNasi wrote down the oral tradition of the law in the late second century AD. This written oral tradition is known as the Mishnah. It represents rabbinical interpretation and application of the laws found in the Torah.

Though the date of its writing is late second century, the oral tradition it contains is thought to be hundreds of years older. It can safely be assumed that many of its teachings were consistent with Jewish rabbinical teaching in the days of Jesus and St. Paul.

marriage and family

When sexual ethics are presented in the New Testament, particularly by St. Paul, they do not merely echo the ethics of the Old Testament or the Jewish Mishnah. Christian teachings on sex and marriage are markedly different than what was taught among the Jews. Judaism allowed and even promoted polygamy and concubines. Many of Israel's most famous Old Testament patriarchs had multiple wives and concubines. Abraham fathered a son from his wife Sarah and from her servant Hagar whom she gave to Abraham as a concubine. Jacob, Abraham's grandson, was married to two women, Rachel and Leah, both of whom gave their servants to Jacob to bear children. King David had at least four wives; Solomon had seven hundred wives and three hundred concubines. Though it was not consistent with God's original design for marriage in the Garden of Eden, multiple wives and concubines were not forbidden by God in the Old Testament. Of course, it should also be said that God never instructed men to take multiple wives either. However, as difficult as it may be for our culture to understand, God did allow people to practice polygamy. The effects of polygamy on family life were debilitating at times. Rachel and Leah's relationship was marked by decades of jealously and ill will. Solomon's many wives are credited with bringing idolatry into Israel. Hagar treated Sarah with contempt after the birth of Ishmael. If Paul's ethical views were merely parroting traditional Jewish practices, then Paul would have promoted husbands taking more than one lifelong sexual partner. He does not.

When Paul speaks of marriage, he speaks in terms of God's original design of one husband to one wife in the Garden of Eden. In 1 Corinthians, Paul says, "Because of the temptation to sexual immorality, each man should have his own wife and each woman her own husband" (1 Corinthians 7:2). His language points to monogamy, one husband with one wife. Paul's words assume that there will not be other partners competing for the affections of the husband but that each husband will be wholly devoted to a single woman and a woman to a single man. It is a direction different from many Old Testament examples (recognizing of course that the greatest example of marriage in the Old Testament is that which God personally created in Adam and Eve and which was clearly monogamous). The principles of marriage and family espoused in the Mishnah, on the other hand, proceeded from an assumption of polygamy.

Despite the practice of having more than one wife, Jewish views on marriage and family still tended to be more respectful toward women than Roman views. One can see tender examples of love and compassion between Old Testament patriarchs and their wives. Abraham and Jacob abided by the will of their wives who gave them servants as concubines. When jealousy arose between Hagar and Sarah, Abraham showed respect and deference to Sarah by listening to her and sending Hagar away. Abraham, Isaac, and Jacob all treated their wives with respect. Wives were not seen as a step above servants nor were they shut up in their homes as Roman women were. In fact, in one of the more detailed descriptions of a good wife, the Old Testament book of Proverbs lauds a wife who buys and sells property, engages in business, and manages the servants. She is praised for her strength, dignity, and wisdom (Proverbs 31). The Old Testament holds womanhood in high regard, as does St. Paul when he speaks of marriage and family.

Before we look at specific matters within the Mishnah, we should note that there were other commentaries on Jewish law circulating among the Jews following the writing of the Mishnah. The Tosephta is a commentary on the Mishnah written shortly after the Mishnah. It does not carry the same authority as the Mishnah, but it does represent the thoughts of rabbis as they applied the laws codified within the Mishnah. Its exact date is unknown, but many believe it to be written sometime in the third century AD. The Tosephta mirrors the Mishnah in many aspects of sexual ethics, and it does give voice to an attitude among certain rabbis that shows a highly negative view of women.

> Rabbi Judah says: There are three Benedictions which one must say every day: Blessed be He who did not make me a Gentile; Blessed be He who did not make me a woman; Blessed be He who did not make me an uneducated man. Blessed be He who did not make me a Gentile. All the nations (Gentiles) are as nothing before Him. Blessed be He who did not make me a woman, for a woman is under no obligation to keep the

commandments. Blessed be He who did not make me an uneducated person, for no uneducated person fears sin.[1]

Again, one might argue that such a document that dates probably to the
third century is inadmissible in discovering first-century attitudes about
women, but there seems little doubt that such "benedictions" predate the
rabbi who gives them voice. The thrust of his argument, that women
were not under the law to the same degree as men, also seems to be a
principle at work within the Mishnah and therefore within the earlier
oral tradition. At a minimum, this statement shows a persistent inequality in the Jewish mind between men and women extending over several
hundred years.

Over time, groups of rabbis gathered their understanding of the
Mishnah into writings known as the Talmud. The Talmud represents
numerous volumes of rabbinical commentary on the Mishnah. Two
Talmuds arose over time: the Jerusalem Talmud (AD 400) and the Babylonian Talmud (AD 500). The Babylonian is much longer than the Jerusalem and is recognized as the more authoritative of the two. When
compared with the Mishnah, the Talmud does not show much progres-
sion in appreciation for womanhood. Old laws and attitudes are essentially unchanged. In tractate Sanhedrin of the Babylonian Talmud, one
group of rabbis teaches the following:

> A daughter is a vain treasure to her father: through anxiety on
> her account, he cannot sleep at night. As a minor, lest she be
> seduced; in her majority, lest she play the harlot; as an adult,
> lest she be not married; if she marries, lest she bear no chil-
> dren; if she grows old, lest she engage in witchcraft! But the
> Rabbis have said the same: The world cannot exist without
> males and females; happy is he whose children are males, and
> woe to him whose children are females.[2]

Certainly, not every Jewish man thought of women in these terms,
but the inclusion in the Talmud of such sayings shows these ideas were
accepted by a good number of rabbis. Whether this was a teaching in

---

[1] *Tractate Berakoth, "Benedictions," Mishna and Tosephta*, trans. A. Lukyn Williams (New
York: The MacMillan Co., 1921), 84, section vii, 18.

[2] Rabbi Isidore Epstein, ed., "Sanhedrin 100b," trans. H. Freedman, in *Soncino
Hebrew/English Babylonian Talmud* (Jew's College online ed.," www.come-and-
hear.com/sanhedrin/sanhedrin_100.html) (accessed February 1, 2016).

Paul's day is impossible to determine. The value of this passage lies in its demonstration that negative attitudes about women persisted in writing for three centuries after the Mishnah and were consistent with attitudes present in the oral tradition of the rabbis who would have lived contemporaneously with Paul. A view of womanhood as less than men was entrenched within Jewish teachings. Marriage was not a union of equals, and women were, in large part, the sexual property of men. Paul's doctrine broke with Jewish cultural attitudes. As he described marriage, he treats women with a much higher regard and gives them equal importance within the family.

divorce

The lesser status of women is evident in divorce laws laid out in the Mishnah—laws that are weighted decidedly toward the man. A man can divorce his wife for virtually any reason according to the Mishnah:

> The school of Shammai says: A man may not divorce his wife unless he has found unchastity in her, for it is written, *Because he has found in her* indecency *in anything.* And the school of Hillel say, [He may divorce her] even if she spoiled a dish for him, for it is written, *Because he has found in her indecency in anything.* R. Akiba says: Even if he found another fairer than she, for it is written, *And it shall be that if she find no favour in his eyes.*[3]

The debate between the schools of Shammai and Hillel seems to have been won by the school of Hillel. Divorce for any reason was the practice in Israel. All a man needed to do to divorce his wife was to give her a signed and dated writ of divorce with the appropriate signatures of witnesses that said, "Lo, thou art free to marry any man."[4] Reasons for the divorce were not necessary. This was the debate into which the Pharisees tried to drag Jesus:

> And Pharisees came up to him and tested him by asking, "Is it lawful to divorce one's wife for any cause?" He answered,

---

[3] Herbert Danby ed., "Gittin 9:10," in *The Mishnah* (Oxford: Oxford University Press, 1933), 321. © Oxford University Press.

[4] Danby, "Gittin 9:3," in *The Mishnah,* 319. © Oxford University Press.

"Have you not read that he who created them from the beginning made them male and female, and said, 'Therefore a man shall leave his father and his mother and hold fast to his wife, and the two shall become one flesh'? So they are no longer two but one flesh. What therefore God has joined together, let not man separate." They said to him, "Why then did Moses command one to give a certificate of divorce and to send her away?" He said to them, "Because of your hardness of heart Moses allowed you to divorce your wives, but from the beginning it was not so. And I say to you: whoever divorces his wife, except for sexual immorality, and marries another, commits adultery." (Matthew 19:3–9)

Jesus treats marriage as a sacred gift of God not to be broken unless the pledge of sexual fidelity had been violated. In that regard, His answer is closer to the school of Shammai than of Hillel. That Jesus answered the Pharisees by pointing to Adam and Eve supports the point that New Testament Christianity did not shape its view on marriage from the examples of polygamy found among the Old Testament patriarchs, or on Jewish oral tradition, but on the original intent for marriage as designed by God in Eden.

no equal justice

In her book *Chattel or Person*, Judith Romney Wegner writes:

From the standpoint of women's personhood, the most conspicuous feature of these rules (regarding marriage and divorce) is their one-sidedness. The wife's lack of corresponding rights against the husband reflects a polygynous system in which the wife is the husband's exclusive sexual property, but the reverse is not the case. Even the ceremonial formalities of marriage and divorce, expressing the husband's acquisition of disposition of the wife, emphasize the biblical-mishnaic view of the wife's sexuality as the husband's property.[5]

---

[5] Judith Romney Wegner, *Chattel or Person? The Status of Women in the Mishnah* (New York: Oxford University Press, 1988), 15.

It is true that marriage law in both the Old Testament and rabbinic Judaism gave rights to males (both husbands and fathers) that were not given to women. The law made women responsible to men and gave men rights over women as their sexual property. As pointed out earlier, however, the example of the Old Testament patriarchs was not one of dominance over women. They modelled respect, honor, and love within their marriages. The Old Testament patriarchs do not stand as examples of men who abused the law by repressing their wives. We see many examples in the Old Testament of husbands listening to their wives and respecting their wishes and their wisdom.[6]

The oral tradition of the Jews shows a lesser regard for the position of women within the family. A woman's purpose was to provide heirs for her husband. The Mishnah says that men should have at least two children. If his first wife does not produce a child within ten years, he is encouraged to seek heirs by taking a second wife.[7] Under the principles put forward by the rabbinic school of Hillel, he could divorce his first wife and marry another; or under the rules of Shammai, he could keep his first wife and simply add a second. Whichever he chose was within his legal rights. The will of the wife was not considered to be a necessary part of his decision under the law. The Mishnah states that the law to be fruitful and multiply fell to the man, not the woman.

St. Paul broke with the teachings of the Jewish rabbis. For example, a woman's value was not tied to her ability to have children. She was equally valuable in the marriage with or without children. The divine command to be fruitful and multiply was not an absolute rule given strictly to men. In a truly remarkable passage that will be examined in more detail in the next chapter, Paul gives women the same sexual rights within the marriage as he gives men. "For the wife does not have authority over her own body, but the husband does. Likewise the husband does not have authority over his own body, but the wife does" (1 Corinthians 7:4). In the New Testament, the man and the woman have equal rights to each other's sexual attention whether or not children are the ultimate fruit of that attention. Paul does not advocate a feminist view of equality in all things. Men have certain roles to serve and women have others. The sexes are not interchangeable in temporal duties in the New Testament, but this in no way suggests that one sex is inferior or lesser than the other.

---

[6] Cf. Genesis 16:3; Judges 13:8–11, 23; Ruth 3:8–13; 1 Samuel 25:32–35; Esther 7.

[7] Danby, "Yebamoth 6:6," in *The Mishnah*, 227.

Both sexes are equally important to God and are to be equally respected as they fulfil their unique roles within the marriage. That understanding parted ways with popular opinions in both Roman and Jewish culture.

levirate marriage

There are other views on sex, like levirate marriage, that are unique to the Jews and find no corresponding expression in St. Paul's teachings. The idea of levirate marriage comes from Deuteronomy 25:5–10. It holds that if a man who has no male heir dies, his brother should take his widow as a wife and father a son in his brother's name. This is a much-discussed topic in the Mishnah with many pages of possible scenarios explored.[8] For example,

> If there were two [married] brothers and the first one died [childless], and the second took in levirate marriage his deceased brother's wife; and afterward a [third] brother was born and then second brother died; the wife of the first brother is exempt [from levirate marriage with the third brother] in that she was "the wife of his brother who did not live at the same time as he," and the wife of the second brother is exempt in that she was her co-wife. If the second brother had only bespoken her for himself and then died, his [first] wife must perform *halitzah* and may not contract levirate marriage [with the third brother]. R Simeon says: He may contract levirate marriage with which of them he will, or submit to *halitzah* from which of them he will.[9]

The need to perpetuate the name of a brother is tied to the tribal mindset of ancient Israel. Establishing lines of descent through generations was essential to establishing one's place among the people of God. Unbroken lines of descent were evidence that this or that family rightly belonged to the chosen people. Clear family trees were also necessary for establishing the legitimacy of the Messianic line.

Paul is sent primarily to the Gentiles, who were never part of the chosen people. The old tribal mentality simply did not apply to them. Nor, indeed, did it apply to anyone after the coming of Christ. The

---

[8] Cf. Danby, "Yebamoth," in *The Mishnah*, 218f.

[9] Danby, "Yebamoth 2:2," in *The Mishnah*, 219. © Oxford University Press.

Messiah redefined the nature of the people of God. Israel is no longer identified by biological family trees, but by inclusion within the grace and eternal life given by Christ. So St. Paul tells the Romans, "For not all who are descended from Israel belong to Israel, and not all are children of Abraham because they are his offspring, but 'Through Isaac shall your offspring be named.' This means that it is not the children of the flesh who are the children of God, but the children of the promise are counted as offspring" (Romans 9:6–8). This new definition of the people of God had a direct impact on marriage. The need to establish tribal descent through levirate marriage became irrelevant. So, when Paul speaks of a wife's husband dying, he says that she is released from the law and may marry whomever she wants (Romans 7:2–3; 1 Corinthians 7:39). The entire concept of levirate marriage is never promoted in the New Testament.

Virginity and purity

Jewish law expresses great concern with purity in regard to a woman's virginity. This concern is found both in the Old Testament (Deuteronomy 22:13–21) and the Mishnah.[10] A new bride's purity was of such importance that if she were found not to be a virgin, she was punished with death (Deuteronomy 22:20–21). In the Mishnah, allowance is made for unusual cases where a woman's lack of virginity may be the result of an accident that ruptured her hymen.[11] Beyond the unique circumstance of such an accident, a man had a legal right to expect his new bride would be a virgin. There is no corresponding concern about the virginity of the husband.

Not only was a new bride's virginity to be expected, but it was also protected. If a new bride was wrongly accused by her husband of losing her virginity prior to the marriage, the husband would be punished with a fine and forbidden from ever divorcing his wife (Deuteronomy 22:13–19). Raping a virgin was a serious crime. If the woman was betrothed to another man and she protested her rape, the rapist was to be stoned to death. If she did not protest the rape, then both parties were to be stoned. If the virgin who was raped was not betrothed to another man, then the

---

[10] Danby, "Ketuboth 1:6–7," in *The Mishnah*, 246.
[11] Danby, "Ketuboth 1:6–7," in *The Mishnah*, 246.

rapist was to marry her and would never be able to divorce her (Deuteronomy 22:28–29).

In every case, the virginity of the woman was treated as a matter of great importance. If she gave her virginity away willingly outside of marriage, there were penalties imposed on her. If her virginity was taken from her, there were penalties imposed on the male. Yet, it does beg the question as to why the concern for virginity is so one-sided? Why is it that only the woman's virginity mattered? Some might accuse Judaism of sexism because only women were held accountable for their virginity, but others see this as womanhood being held in high regard. Her womb is considered the seat of life from which comes beings created in the image of God. Life is sacred and the place where life is formed is to be treated as sacred space. It was protected under the full force of the law, including even the penalty of death.

While respecting the sacredness of human life and the place of its formation, the New Testament does not treat women differently when it comes to loss of virginity. The expectation for sexual purity is equally important for men and women. Warnings against fornication and impure behavior are applied to both sexes.[12] The New Testament differs as well in the final definition of purity. Being pure no longer belongs to physical evidences of virginity as defined by the law. One becomes pure by an act of Christ. This includes even sexual purity. A passage we will examine more closely in the next chapter is 1 Corinthians 6:9–11. It speaks to the purifying power of Christ's forgiving grace,

> Or do you not know that the unrighteous will not inherit the kingdom of God? Do not be deceived: neither the sexually immoral, nor idolaters, nor adulterers, nor men who practice homosexuality, nor thieves, nor the greedy, nor drunkards, nor revilers, nor swindlers will inherit the kingdom of God. And such were some of you. But you were washed, you were sanctified, you were justified in the name of the Lord Jesus Christ and by the Spirit of our God.

The images of washing and being sanctified (made holy) are purity images. In Christ, purity does not rest in the physical reality the person

---

[12] Cf. Romans 13:11–14; 1 Corinthians 7:2; Ephesians 5:3; Hebrews 13:4; 1 Thessalonians 4:1–8.

brings to God, but in the new creation God works within the person. Forgiveness restores purity in God's eyes.

Not surprisingly, then, when Jesus is confronted by a legal case of sexual impurity, which by the standards of the Old Testament law should have been punishable by death, He redirects the punishment to grace.

> The scribes and the Pharisees brought a woman who had been caught in adultery, and placing her in the midst they said to him, "Teacher, this woman has been caught in the act of adultery. Now in the Law Moses commanded us to stone such women. So what do you say?" This they said to test him, that they might have some charge to bring against him. Jesus bent down and wrote with his finger on the ground. And as they continued to ask him, he stood up and said to them, "Let him who is without sin among you be the first to throw a stone at her." And once more he bent down and wrote on the ground. But when they heard it, they went away one by one, beginning with the older ones, and Jesus was left alone with the woman standing before him. Jesus stood up and said to her, "Woman, where are they? Has no one condemned you?" She said, "No one, Lord." And Jesus said, "Neither do I condemn you; go, and from now on sin no more." (John 8:3–11)

Jesus does not dispute the fact that the woman violated the moral law, and by telling her to go and sin no more, He upholds the moral requirement of chastity, but forgiveness takes the place of the strict demand for civil punishment. He removed the legal condemnation against her and assumed it within Himself. By His death on the cross, she was set free from the punishment the law demanded. She was given an imputed purity—a purity via the washing away of sin through an act of Christological substitution. Under the law, she had been found impure, but under Jesus' grace, He faced punishment for her and thus removed the legal condemnation against her sexual impurity.

The same principle can be seen in the story from Luke 7, where a woman who was a known prostitute washed Jesus' feet with her tears and dried them with her hair. Her actions were offensive to the Pharisee at whose home Jesus was eating. He questioned what kind of prophet Jesus was to let such a woman touch Him. Jesus' response to the woman and to the Pharisee's criticism was to forgive her. He restored her to the love of

God by removing the offense of her sexual impurity. He essentially redefined her life in light of the new purity of grace that covered her.

This is not to suggest that sexual chastity was no longer important to New Testament Christians. In the next chapter, there will be a number of passages discussed that show how Christians valued sexual chastity. The application of grace to cover unchaste behavior and to remove the legal demands of punishment for sins against virginity is not a free license to sin. It is instead the giving of a superior kind of purity that both forgives sin and empowers individuals to live holier lives more devoted to God and His will. Christians who receive grace care about being chaste because they have been joined to the purity of Christ.

sex and children

It is surprising how the Mishnah addresses the sexual abuse of children. In Ketuboth 1:3, the penalties for sex with children are a mere fine. If an adult male had sex with a girl under the age of three or a boy under nine had intercourse with an adult woman, a fine of two hundred denars is imposed.[13] The Mishnah does not seem to be promoting sexual abuse of children, but the fact that the penalty for such abuse is so small is shocking, especially when it is recognized that it may be a child under age 3 that was abused! The lack of harsher penalties sends a message that sexual child abuse is not a serious crime. The penalties for the rape of an adult are more severe than for the rape of children. The Mishnah allows for men to be married to minors,[14] and, presumably, to have sexual relations with them.

There is no age of consent given in the New Testament, but its overwhelming testimony is that marriage is a union between one man and one woman who are sexually mature and able to decide to commit to each other for life. Pederasty and paedophilia are condemned and forbidden under general prohibitions against uncleanness and fornication.[15]

---

[13] Danby, "Ketuboth 1:3," in *The Mishnah*, 245. "If he that was of age had connexion with her that was a minor [footnote: Less than three years and a day], or if he that was a minor [footnote: Less than nine years and a day] had connexion with her that was of age or, through accident, not *virgo intacta*, her *Ketubah* is 200 denars." © Oxford University Press.

[14] Danby, "Gittin 5:5," in *The Mishnah*, 313. Cf. "Gittin 6:3," 314–315.

[15] For example, 1 Corinthians 6:17–20; cf. Ephesians 5:3–8. Daniel Heimbach rightly observes that sexual intercourse between adults and children does not need the explicit disapproval of Scripture because the Bible thoroughly excludes the idea implicitly through the broader application of texts dealing with marriage, chastity and the protection of

Homosexuality

Among the many instructions on sexual conduct God gave the Israelites are strict prohibitions against homosexuality. Two main passages are cited: Leviticus 18:22, "You shall not lie with a male as with a woman; it is an abomination"; and Leviticus 20:13, "If a man lies with a male as with a woman, both of them have committed an abomination; they shall surely be put to death; their blood is upon them." In addition, Deuteronomy states: "None of the daughters of Israel shall be a cult prostitute, and none of the sons of Israel shall be a cult prostitute" (23:17). The "cult prostitute," especially the male, would have been homosexual in nature. All prostitution was forbidden. The story of God's judgment on Sodom and Gomorrah (Genesis 19) shows God's opinion of unrepentant homosexual sins, as does the story of the same sins being perpetrated by the men of Gibeah against a traveling Levite (Judges 19:22). The sins of the men of Gibeah resulted in a civil war that nearly destroyed the entire tribe of Benjamin. Jewish oral tradition in Paul's day followed the strict letter of Old Testament law. In Sanhedrin 7:4, the Mishnah condemns homosexual acts in the same breath as sex with animals and restates the necessity for the death penalty.[16]

Paul's treatment of homosexuality in the New Testament differs from the Old Testament in two important ways. First, there is no mention in the New Testament of a continuation of the civil punishment for homosexual sins; there is no death sentence. Second, as homosexual sins are addressed to the Roman cities, they are often lumped in with other sins and are treated in the same manner as other sins. Same-sex sins are the same as stealing, idolatry, and heterosexual sins. What this ultimately means is that they are as forgivable as those other sins and as damning if there is no repentance.

All sexual conduct, homosexual or heterosexual, is treated as a matter of moral law by the New Testament. In the following chapter, there is a more detailed discussion of how moral law differs from both civil and ceremonial law for the Jews. For now, we simply note that moral law is understood as applicable to all human beings and is neither time bound

---

children from corruption. Daniel R. Heimbach, *True Sexual Morality: Recovering Biblical Standards for a Culture in Crisis* (Wheaton, IL: Crossway Books, 2004), 194–195.

[16] Danby, "Sanhedrin 7:4," in *The Mishnah*, 392. "He that has connexion with a male or with a beast, and she that suffers connexion with a beast, [there death is] by stoning." © Oxford University Press.

nor culturally specific. Violations of moral law within the New Testament are not met with prescribed civil punishments. Any physical/civil punishments to be meted out for violations of the moral law are either the responsibility of the local secular government or are relegated to God's ultimate judgment. New Testament Christians are responsible for the moral law, as were Old Testament Jews. The difference between the New and the Old lies in the nature of this responsibility. In Judaism the responsibility was founded on the law and its threats. Obedience was expected because God demanded it. Violations of the law were met with swift justice. The oral tradition of the Jews was an attempt to explain various details and applications of the divine law. However, in explaining matters of application, the oral tradition expanded the law, creating new and more complex laws. Jews were bound not only to the letter of the Old Testament law, but to the complexities of the oral tradition. As that applied to homosexual sins, the law was clear that death was the only acceptable outcome.

The nature of obedience for Christians was radically different. The same biblical laws were in play, but obedience for Christians flowed from two sources, God's Law and His Gospel. Instead of obedience only seen as a demand under the Law, Christians saw obedience as a new freedom under the Gospel—they were set free to obey. The moral law became an expression of the new holier life given them by God's Spirit. They were not compelled to obey God's Law simply by threats; they were set free to obey through their reconciliation with God. The moral law was not only an obligation; it was a natural expression of the holiness of God given to them. One can see this in Paul's letter to the Romans:

> Likewise, my brothers, you also have died to the law through the body of Christ, so that you may belong to another, to him who has been raised from the dead, in order that we may bear fruit for God. For while we were living in the flesh, our sinful passions, aroused by the law, were at work in our members to bear fruit for death. But now we are released from the law, having died to that which held us captive, so that we serve in the new way of the Spirit and not in the old way of the written code. (Romans 7:4–6)

Similar thoughts are found in Paul's letter to the Ephesians:

For by grace you have been saved through faith. And this is not your own doing; it is the gift of God, not a result of works, so that no one may boast. For we are his workmanship, created in Christ Jesus for good works, which God prepared beforehand, that we should walk in them. (Ephesians 2:8–10)

Both Jews and Christians would have been concerned about sexual morality, but for very different reasons. Jews living under the oral tradition and the strict letter of Old Testament civil law would have pursued morality out of compulsion. Violations would be cause for fear and met with immediate punishment. Christians wanted to be moral because they were new creations in the grace of Christ. They knew there was full forgiveness with God for past moral failures. They sought chastity as a new freedom under grace, not because of fear under the hammer of the law. Christians knew that those who refused to repent and insisted on maintaining an immoral life would face God's judgment. The early Christians were not anti-law. Obedience was a constant concern, but the Gospel was a greater force than the Law in creating a love for obedience within them. It forgave all moral transgressions, placed people into the salvation of Christ, and empowered people to live holier lives in keeping with the will of God. As this relates to sexuality, Christians saw each other's maleness or femaleness in terms of their joint relationship to Christ, not in terms of following the rules of rabbinic law. They saw the sexual relationship as an expression of self-emptying love and fidelity in the image of their Savior whose single-minded devotion to them led Him to sacrifice His life on their behalf. The next chapter will demonstrate that Gospel, not the rabbinic law, was the foundation for Christian views on sex.

chapter 3

VERSES EXAMINED

revisiting context

The role of context in determining meaning looms large when it comes to interpreting specific verses of the Bible. To understand sexual ethics as discussed in the Bible, it helps immensely to know something about the views of sex in first-century culture. It is also necessary to understand the overall teaching of the New Testament and what other issues each writer may have been addressing that relate to the topic of sexuality. Going further, each verse must be read in the context of the verses around it and there must be proper definitions of individual words. The study of context takes on a nesting box structure, where each individual layer of context fits into another layer clarifying the intended meaning of the author.

A word standing on its own without a clear context is virtually impossible to understand. For example, the word *post* on its own can mean a metal rod placed in the dirt for support, a wooden stake, a piece of mail, a line where a race begins, to fasten something where it can be seen by others, a place where soldiers are stationed, to make a deposit, a system of mail transfer, and "after." Which meaning the word *post* has in a particular sentence will be determined by the context around it.

So we might find *post* in a sentence: "He walked to the post." This narrows the meaning of the word *post*, but does not yet give us an exact definition. We can be sure a noun is meant and can eliminate the meanings that are not nouns. It could be a wooden or metal stake, a starting line, a piece of mail, or a place where soldiers are stationed. Expanding the context will help gain more clarity. "He walked to the post. After kicking it, he bent over and picked it up." Now we can eliminate all nouns that cannot be picked up, like a line at the beginning of a race or a soldiers' station. *Post* must mean either a stake or rod used for support or a piece of mail. "He walked to the post. After kicking it, he bent over and picked it up. Then he pounded it into the ground." Broadening the context gives more meaning. Now we know we are talking about a rod or stake used for support. If we note that the chapter of the book in which this sentence is found is "A Hundred Uses for Metal Stakes," we get a better idea of the kind of stake being pounded. If we see that the subsection of the chapter in which the sentence occurs is "The Mysterious Red T-stake," then we get an even better understanding of exactly what kind of stake is being used. The more context we can add to the discussion, the more certain we can be of the meaning.

In the following pages, it is my goal to examine layers of context that might help better explain the meaning of individual verses addressing sexual conduct and attitudes. We began with the broad context of culture and social practice in Paul's day. From there it is necessary to focus on individual books, chapters, verses, and words. Each level of context will help clarify meaning and provide a more certain understanding of what the apostle was saying.

Context is sometimes purposely ignored in order to define words in such a way that one side gains an advantage. I have had several conversations with proponents of sexual hedonism who defined words with meanings that were unlikely or even impossible in the given context. As an example, the Sixth Commandment says, "You shall not commit adultery." Normally, we read this as a broad statement, "You should not have sexual intercourse of any kind with anyone except your spouse." But some have argued that the word for "to commit adultery" (Greek *moicheuo*, μοιχεύω, or *moichao*, μοιχάω) only describes sexual intercourse of a married person with someone who is not his or her spouse. Therefore, they say, it is a term only applied to married people, not single people. Indeed, if one traces the history of this word, there is justification to say that it did mean "cheating on a spouse" and therefore was referring to married people. But the question is not what did the word mean once upon a time, but how was the word *adultery* understood when it was used by Jesus or Paul. Did they mean it as applicable only to married people cheating on spouses, or did they use this word in a broader sense to include even the unmarried? To answer that, one needs to look at the broader context.

How is this word used throughout the New Testament? Are there other words or expressions used in proximity to this word that clarify it? Are there other passages that explain the Sixth Commandment that might show God's intent is not just the sexual exclusivity of spouses once married but the limitation of all sexual activity to the marriage union?

The words *moicheuo* and *moichao* as verbs (to commit adultery or to cause to commit adultery) are found twenty times in the New Testament. In Luke 16:18, Jesus links *moicheuo* to marriage when He says, "Everyone who divorces his wife and marries another commits adultery, and he who marries a woman divorced from her husband commits adultery." Here Jesus is speaking about having intercourse with a woman who is still considered a wife even though the husband may have gotten a legal divorce. However, in Matthew 5:27–28, Jesus uses the word in a way that can be applied beyond marriage. "You have heard that it was said, 'You shall not commit adultery.' But I say to you that everyone who looks at a woman with lustful intent has already committed adultery with her in his heart." This is spoken as part of Jesus' Sermon on the Mount to a large group of people, both married and unmarried, men, women, and children. Jesus expands the traditional meaning of the word to include anyone who looks lustfully at the opposite sex.

The noun *adultery* (*moicheia*, μοιχεία) is used in conjunction with the Greek words for fornication and uncleanness (Matthew 15:19; Mark 7:21; John 8:3; and Galatians 5:19). This suggests that adultery is simply another facet of an overall sexual impurity that Scripture warns against. The greater context of Scripture shows that the prohibition against adultery should be understood as applicable beyond the narrow problem of one spouse cheating on another. It is biblically accurate to teach that the Sixth Commandment, "You shall not commit adultery," does forbid any sexual activity outside of marriage.[1]

We live in a culture that has a vested interest in misinterpreting the passages about sex and morality. Christian teaching stands in the way of prevailing social attitudes about sex. If doubt can be cast on the meaning of God's Word, then a major impediment to sexual hedonism can be removed. During one of my lectures, a student sitting toward the back had

---

[1] Luther's explanation of the Sixth Commandment reflects this broader meaning of the word *adultery*.

an online article on his smartphone written by someone with a PhD (so one would assume that person must know what he or she is talking about). The article cast doubt on the meaning of the words used in 1 Corinthians 6 to condemn homosexuality. He read an excerpt from the article that made the claim that the Greek word normally translated as "homosexual" in 1 Corinthians 6 did not really mean "homosexual." The article singled out the Greek word *malakoi* (singular *malakos*). It claimed that the word really means "soft" and is not a sexual word at all. What Paul was apparently denouncing was "soft" people, which could be people who were overweight and out of shape (so Paul is denouncing gluttony or laziness), or maybe people who dressed in luxurious soft clothing while others dressed in rags (which would mean Paul was denouncing social inequality). The author of the article claimed *malakoi* could mean any number of things and the only reason it was translated as "homosexuals" in 1 Corinthians was because of an anti-homosexual bias in the translators. The argument apparently cinched the debate in the mind of the student reading it.

What the student did not understand was that the writer of the article was making one of the most basic errors in interpretation. He was isolating a word from its context and using its etymology (the origin and history of a word) to define it in a different way than the author intended. Context determines meaning much more than etymology. *Malakos* does mean "soft."[2] Jesus Himself uses this word with reference to clothing in Matthew 11:8, when He asks the crowds who went to John the Baptist, "What then did you go out to see? A man dressed in soft clothing? Behold, those who wear soft clothing are in kings' houses." In 1 Corinthians 6, however, Paul uses this word in the middle of a discussion about sexual practices. The context is not about clothes. In the Roman culture where Paul was talking, the word *soft* often meant a male who played the woman in sexual situations.[3] It is similar to our word *gay*. In the mid-

---

[2] Bauer, Danker, Arndt, Gingrich, *A Greek-English Lexicon of the New Testament and other Early Christian Literature*, 3rd ed. (Chicago: The University of Chicago Press, 2000), 613 (henceforth referred to as BDAG). "1. pert. to being yielding to touch, 'soft' of things: clothes. 2. pert. to being passive in a same-sex relationship, effeminate esp. of catamites, of men and boys who are sodomized by other males in such a relationship."

[3] Williams, *Roman Homosexuality: Ideologies of Masculinity in Classical Antiquity*, 128f. Williams discusses the Latin *mollis*, which means "soft." He shows the term was used as an insult toward men who conducted themselves in womanly ways. This was often seen in their sexual practices with other men, as the partner who was penetrated, but could at times be applied to cross-dressers and eunuchs as well.

Twentieth century and earlier, the word *gay* meant "happy." Now it almost exclusively means "homosexual." At what period in time the word *gay* was used and how the people would have understood it helps determine which meaning it should have.

When we apply contextual considerations to what Paul says in 1 Corinthians 6, there is no doubt that he is talking about homosexuality. In the era when he lived, people would have understood the term *malakoi* as referring to men who were willingly sodomized. The audience to whom Paul was writing often used *malakoi* as a sexual term. In the overall context of 1 and 2 Corinthians, sexual behavior was a reoccurring theme. The main point Paul was discussing in the sentence where this word is found was sexual behavior. There are other terms used on all sides of *malakoi* to indicate that Paul's concern was sexual morality. It is absurd to argue that in the middle of a discourse about sexual behavior Paul would suddenly throw in a condemnation about wearing soft clothing or being out of shape.

In the following pages, the verses in the Bible that will be examined tend to be the main texts used in the debate about sexual conduct. As these are reviewed, it must be remembered that passages are not isolated statements unto themselves, but are part of a greater New Testament concern. Together they form a consistent whole. What Paul says in one place, he repeats in other places. Other apostles and even Jesus Himself repeat the same thoughts. As context expands from word to verse to book of the Bible to the overall teaching of the whole Scripture, we will see a consistent message about a new life of chastity that has been given to us in Christ Jesus.

general passages about marriage

What follows are pertinent texts about marriage written to new Christian converts living in the towns where St. Paul ministered. The people who read these words for the first time were a mix of Jewish and pagan converts. The Jewish converts were raised to accept polygamy and define marriage in legalistic terms. The Gentile converts were raised to accept infidelity in marriage and promiscuity outside of marriage. Paul's teachings elevated marriage to a status unknown by Jews or Romans. He taught a profound form of love between husband and wife that is born from the saving grace of Christ.

These passages form the substance of the Christian witness to the hedonistic world in which they lived. Paul taught the Christians both to believe the truth of what he said personally and to live by those principles in the midst of the promiscuous world around them. My experience in the secular classroom has shown that even those who do not consider themselves Christians know the Bible says something prohibiting certain sexual sins. They do not often know the exact words of the passages and certainly do not understand how prohibitions of the law interact with pronouncements of grace, but they do know the Christian Bible says something that disagrees with a hedonistic mindset.

This actually provides an opportunity for Christians who are familiar with a deeper understanding of the biblical text to teach non-Christians. Even though secular people will not think the Bible is any more holy or inspired than another religion's book, they have, in my experience, at least shown a willingness to listen to a Christian's explanation of the text. As these various passages formed the basis of the early Christian witness about sexual morality, they still form the foundation for the Christian witness today.

1 CORINTHIANS 7:2-5

> But because of the temptation to sexual immorality, each man should have his own wife and each woman her own husband. The husband should give to his wife her conjugal rights, and likewise the wife to her husband. For the wife does not have authority over her own body, but the husband does. Likewise the husband does not have authority over his own body, but the wife does. Do not deprive one another, except perhaps by agreement for a limited time, that you may devote yourselves to prayer; but then come together again, so that Satan may not tempt you because of your lack of self-control.

The word translated above as "sexual immorality" in Greek is *porneias* (πορνείας). It is a plural word that is better translated "sexual immoralities."[4] It is the same word from which we get the English word *porn*, and it means roughly the same thing. The origin of the word shows

---

[4] Cf. Gregory Lockwood, *Concordia Commentary: 1 Corinthians* (St. Louis: Concordia, 2000), 228–229. Lockwood points out that the use of the plural emphasizes the multiplicity of sexual sins so prevalent in Corinth.

that it came from the Greek word *pernemi* (πέρνημι), "to sell," and thus was originally attached to the idea of prostitution.[5] As it is used in the New Testament, however, the meaning is broader and involves any sort of fornication (sex outside of marriage) or immorality. In the passage above, Paul's concern is not merely for people being tempted to hire prostitutes, but for people who are tempted to engage in sexual activity outside of the marriage bond.

There is a clear monogamous exclusivity here: "each man should have his own wife and each woman her own husband." The sense of the word *have* seems to point to sexual relations: "having a spouse in the fullest sense."[6] Christian marriage is between one man and one woman and is to be the exclusive place where one's sexual desires are met. Polygamy is ruled out because the wife is to have authority over her husband's sexuality. In a polygamous relationship, that authority could not belong to one wife. All wives would have to share this authority and thus a power struggle over control of the husband's affection would be created. This situation clearly does not fit with the harmonious union Paul describes as marriage.

This passage is also valuable in the discussion over same-sex marriage. Paul's image of the marriage union is one man bound to one woman, each with exclusive rights to the sexual expression of the other. One cannot argue that Paul did not know about homosexual relationships, and that is why he frames the marriage relation in traditional terms of opposite genders. It was established in chapter 1 that same-sex relationships were common throughout the Roman Empire in Paul's day. Nero's same-sex marriage came very late in his rule (possibly AD 67)—well after Paul had written Romans and 1 Corinthians. Yet the culture of Paul's day was accepting of homosexual relations to the point that it set the stage for Nero's marriage to a man. When Paul says that in marriage "each man should have his own wife and each woman her own husband," he is consciously limiting sexual activity to opposite-sex couples in marriage and making a statement against prevailing social attitudes.

If we look beyond the immediate context of St. Paul's letters, we find marriage being defined in terms of one man and one women on the lips of Jesus Himself.

---

[5] Gerhard Kittle, *Theological Dictionary of the New Testament*, vol. 6, trans. Geoffrey W. Bromiley (Grand Rapids, MI: Eerdmans, 1988), 580.

[6] Lockwood, *1 Corinthians*, 229.

> And Pharisees came up to him and tested him by asking, "Is it lawful to divorce one's wife for any cause?" He answered, "Have you not read that he who created them from the beginning made them male and female, and said, 'Therefore a man shall leave his father and his mother and hold fast to his wife, and the two shall become one flesh'?" (Matthew 19:3–5)

When Jesus spoke of marriage, He began at the beginning with the creation of male and female. God did not just make Adam and Eve as separate beings. He created them as different genders and joined them together in the special bond of marriage. Whenever the Bible speaks of marriage as God designed it, it always and without exception assumes a male/female bond. Even though the pagan culture of Rome, which was the dominant world culture at the time, allowed for same-sex unions and even, in Nero's case, same-sex marriage, Christians continued to confess that marriage should be between one man and one woman because that was God's original design.

Returning to 1 Corinthians 7:2–5, Paul stresses sexual exclusivity as an expectation for the followers of Christ. Husband and wife would only know intercourse with each other. This stood in contrast to Roman sexual promiscuity, which was driven by the man's need to express his Roman sense of strength and domination. This principle of being devoted exclusively to one person for life indirectly accused the prevailing culture of sin. If intercourse was acceptable to God only in the context of a man and woman with each other in marriage, then any sexual activity outside of this context was wrong, which meant many of the socially acceptable sexual practices of the majority of Romans were wrong. As one familiar with human nature, Paul knew that such a statement would draw the displeasure of the Roman majority. It would set his tiny Christian flock against society and in the position of being the object of hostility and ridicule. Yet, finding acceptance from the prevailing culture was not Paul's concern. He knew that as the world hated Jesus, so it would hate His followers who were faithful to God's Word.

The level of sexual equality in Paul's words was also remarkable for the time. Paul addressed men and women on the same terms. The man was to have his own wife as the woman was to have her own husband. Both husband and wife had authority over the other's body. In both Roman and rabbinical Jewish law, the woman's sexuality was essentially under the authority of the husband. Within these traditions, the woman had no equal corresponding authority over her husband's body as she did under Christianity.

The Greek word Paul used for "authority," *exousia* (ἐξουσία), can be defined as: (1) a state of control over something, freedom of choice, right (e.g., the right to act, decide, or dispose of one's property as one wishes); (2) potential or resource to command, control, or govern; capability; might; power; (3) the right to control or command, authority, absolute power, warrant.[7] This seems at first to be the language of "ownership" that was the common view of Roman and Jewish models for the husband's relationship over his wife. When it came to the procreative act, the woman was essentially the property of the man. He had authority over her to produce children. Through Paul's epistles, God revealed a view that was radically different from prevailing views. He applied *exousia* equally in both directions. The woman had the same authority over her husband that the husband had over her in the procreative act. She had a God-given right to demand his exclusive attention. His body was not his own to do with as he wanted. She had control over his sexual actions.

Among the Romans, sex was a physical act that did not necessitate any deeper mental, emotional, or spiritual connection. When they described sexual relationships with young boys or adolescents, then they spoke in terms of deeper mental connections, but with women or slaves, the emotional, intellectual union was not a concern. Intercourse with women was a necessary act to produce children. It was not a union between two equal people. Sex was the Roman male's expressive act of power, not so in Paul's epistles.

The reshaping of the idea of power or authority over others is seen throughout this section of 1 Corinthians 7. Verse 3 stated, "The husband should give to his wife her conjugal rights." The literal reading of this passage in the Greek text is "to the woman, the man should give up what is owed." Sexual relations were a debt of love owed to the other, not an act of the will to be enforced on the other. This shifts the focus from self to the other and makes it an act of self-sacrifice, not an act of selfish taking.

Additionally, God's Word instructs the married couple, "Do not deprive one another, except perhaps by agreement for a limited time." The

---

[7] BDAG, 352–353. Additional meanings include: (4) power exercised by rulers or others in high position by virtue of their office; (5) bearer of ruling authority; (6) the sphere in which power is exercised; (7) a means of exercising power.

stereotypical portrayal of Christians by the Christless world is that Christians avoid sex and prefer celibacy. They believe that Christians see sexual intercourse as inherently evil. Yet here, Scripture clearly encourages regular sexual relations between husband and wife—and not just the physical act of sex, but intercourse with genuine regard for the other person.

As Paul penned these words, he was very conscious of the fact that sexual temptations were strong. He wrote this to people living in Corinth, which was a center for immorality. Corinth was founded by the Dorians around 800 BC. The Dorians, who also founded Sparta, are credited by many sources for making homosexuality culturally acceptable throughout Greece.[8] Being a Corinthian was seen as tantamount to being immoral. The widely accepted reputation of Corinth shows it was an especially difficult place to be sexually chaste.

The congregation at Corinth struggled with this new model of Christian sexual purity. But a healthy sexual relationship between husband and wife would combat the temptation for lust. Should husband or wife refuse intercourse for an extended period of time, Paul recognized that the natural sinful weakness of human flesh could drive the other spouse toward the immorality of the culture in which they lived. For that reason, it was good for husband and wife to be aware of each other's weaknesses and not withhold intercourse for long periods. The one exception he mentions is a mutually agreed upon period of refraining from sexual activity as part of their Christian devotion. Denying oneself in order to focus more on prayer and devotion during penitential times of the Church Year was and still is a good practice.

EPHESIANS 5:22-33

> Wives, submit to your own husbands, as to the Lord. For the husband is the head of the wife even as Christ is the head of the church, his body, and is himself its Savior. Now as the church submits to Christ, so also wives should submit in everything to their husbands. Husbands, love your wives, as Christ loved the church and gave himself up for her, that he might sanctify her, having cleansed her by the washing of water with the word, so that he might present the church to himself in splendor, without spot or wrinkle or any such thing, that she might be holy

---

[8] K. J. Dover, *Greek Homosexuality* (New York: Vintage Books, 1980), 185.

and without blemish. In the same way husbands should love their wives as their own bodies. He who loves his wife loves himself. For no one ever hated his own flesh, but nourishes and cherishes it, just as Christ does the church, because we are members of his body. "Therefore a man shall leave his father and mother and hold fast to his wife, and the two shall become one flesh." This mystery is profound, and I am saying that it refers to Christ and the church. However, let each one of you love his wife as himself, and let the wife see that she respects her husband.

Headship of the husband and submission of the wife were not in and of themselves new ideas. Jewish law placed unmarried women under the authority of their father until such a time as they were married; then authority over her was essentially transferred to her husband. Under Roman tradition, a similar arrangement existed. The *paterfamilias* (father of the family) held authority over all women within his family. A married woman was simply moved to the authority of her new *paterfamilias*. As we have noted, Roman culture was more repressive of women than Jewish culture.

Both Roman and Jewish gender roles were defined by law. Here in Ephesians, Paul's view of submission and headship flows primarily from the Gospel, not the law. St. Paul models the relationship of husband and wife after the relationship of Christ to His Church. The husband is head of his wife as Christ is head of His Church. The wife is submissive to her husband as the Church is submissive to Christ. As Paul explains it, the husband is to bear the image of Christ within the family through self-emptying love and devotion to his wife. It is consistent with the message of the previous passage. This is not male dominance. It is male self-sacrifice. It is placing the needs of the other above one's self. The wife is not submitting to her husband simply because he is male and therefore "the boss," but because he is emptying himself for her in the spirit of Christ. She submits to Christ as Christ manifests himself to her through her husband's love. The Christian definition of headship and submission require both parties in the marriage to be aware of Christ working through them. This is not legalistic "thou shalt" language. This is a new way of looking at the relationship between husband and wife.

This new relationship is in fact a reflection of a very old relationship. Husband and wife are to be to each other as Adam and Eve were to each other. Paul quotes Genesis 2:24, which is God's explanation of the union He originally created. "For this reason a man shall leave his father and mother and be joined to his wife, and the two shall become one flesh." Jesus quotes the same passage. This is a profound thought that speaks of a union exceeding mere emotional attachment. Husband and wife complete each other. Adam and Eve were literally of the same flesh. The decision to form Eve from Adam's rib is a statement about the importance of the woman. This rib was an essential part of Adam that guarded his heart and internal organs. God took a piece of flesh at the center of Adam's body. When Adam told later generations where Eve came from, he would point to the middle of himself. She was literally his center.

It is not insignificant that God allowed Adam a period of being alone before Eve's creation. God let Adam see all the animals and consider how they were all completed by one another. Each male was joined by a female. God allowed Adam to feel alone and to recognize that he was incomplete as a single lonely being. When Eve was brought to Adam, he was more complete with her than he had been without her. She was of his flesh, and he would cherish her as he did his own flesh. This intimate loving relationship established before the fall into sin was a union of two different beings with different roles within the family but of equal importance to each other and to God. The problem of sin did not change God's intent for marriage to complete man and woman in a lifelong union of love and respect. When Paul describes marriage to the Ephesians, he references God's original design with Adam and Eve before the fall.

Paul acknowledges that these are not easy ideas to digest. "This is a great mystery," he says, or as Winger translates in his Ephesians commentary, "This mystery is great."[9] When this mystery is seen through Christian eyes, marriage takes on even greater, more profound dimensions. This union created and defined by God before the fall into sin becomes a union directed by Christ's love after the fall. Husband and wife complete one another as Christ's saving love works within both.

The Ephesians text points to a divine purpose unique to Christian marriage. Marriage for Christians is not simply for the purpose of

---

[9] Thomas Winger, *Concordia Commentary: Ephesians* (St. Louis: Concordia, 2015), 620. Winger explains, "Paul is not saying that it is something that is simply beyond our comprehension, though that is one aspect of μυστήριον, 'mystery.' But as Paul has previously used this key term in Ephesians (1:9; 3:3, 4, 9; later, 6:19), a μυστήριον is something that was once hidden in the mind of God yet has now been disclosed through the revelation of Jesus Christ to his apostolic messengers."

procreation or as a stop against uncontrolled lust. Ephesians binds marriage to Christ's desire to save us. "Husbands, love your wives, as Christ loved the church and gave himself up for her, that [ἵνα] he might sanctify her, having cleansed her by the washing of water with the word, so that [ἵνα] he might present the church to himself in splendor, without spot or wrinkle or any such thing, that [ἵνα] she might be holy and without blemish" (Ephesians 5:25–27). The threefold ἵνα, which the ESV translates as "that" denotes purpose: "in order that."[10] Christ loved the Church for the purpose of saving her, and husbands are to "love your wives, as Christ loved the church."

This goes beyond simply establishing a Christological example for the husband's love of his wife, as if through imitating Christ's self-sacrifice he can fulfill the divine intent for marriage. Eternal life is God's true intent for all people, and as Christ works within husbands and wives, that divine purpose finds unique expression. The purpose of Christ's love is to make the Church holy to God the Father (sanctify her), cleanse her (through the washing of Baptism), and ultimately to bring her to Himself in heaven's splendor. Christian marriage reflects Christ's desire to save His bride. It is not as though a spouse's love can cause the salvation of the other, as Christ's love has saved His people, but that the love Christians have for their spouse extends to the soul. They do what they do for each other with a mind toward strengthening and supporting the other's life within the grace of Christ.

There is a tension of sorts within this Ephesians text between marriage as a human institution and marriage among Christians. Paul's reference to God's design for marriage in Eden presents itself as a pattern for all humanity. The oneness built on love and fidelity between a husband and wife devoted to each other for life is an essential element intended for all marriages. Marital bonds exemplifying mutual respect between one man and one woman are timeless characteristics. To that end, what Ephesians says about a husband's sacrificial love, a wife's submission to her husband, and the spirit of unselfish love between the two is a universal pattern God made applicable to all humanity in every age.

Yet in Ephesians, Paul takes the discussion of marriage into places that only Christians can realize. The fullness of what God intended for marriage includes a Christological concern for the soul of the other. Spouses want their partner to be saved by Christ and want to model the

---

[10] BDAG, 475.

Christological relationship between Christ and His Church because it expresses Christ's salvific love. He sacrificed Himself for the purpose of saving His Church. The husband who models Christ's love for the Church in his relationship with his wife does so for the purpose of supporting Christ's saving work within her. The wife who respects her husband does so for the purpose of exemplifying the Church as the bride of Christ who gladly receives His saving sacrifice. This added Christian dimension to the marriage bond does not negate the more general structure of marriage drawn from Eden; it simply makes Christian marriage a more complete expression of what God designed it to be.

The description of marriage given in Ephesians also has something to say to couples living together before marriage. Sex outside of marriage is harmful to souls. As other passages in this chapter will show, premarital sex and extramarital sex put individuals at odds with God's will, and if they remain in a state of impenitence, they can lose eternal life. Living together before marriage, and therefore having sex before marriage, defeats the Christological character of marriage. Christ intended marriage to reflect His passionate love for the eternal life of His Church, but living together before marriage represents a disregard for the soul of the other. It is sex without the complete investment of oneself in the other. It says, "Yes, God's Word may say this hurts the soul of my partner, but I'm going to do it anyway." True Christ-centered love will put the soul of the other before sexual desires; it will want sex to be more than an act between two people who believe they love each other. It will want intercourse to be a statement of lasting, committed, Christlike love that moves past the flesh and reaches the depth of the soul.

COLOSSIANS 3:18-21

> Wives, submit to your husbands, as is fitting in the Lord. Husbands, love your wives, and do not be harsh with them. Children, obey your parents in everything, for this pleases the Lord. Fathers, do not provoke your children, lest they become discouraged.

Paul presented the same model of Christian marriage to every congregation he served. The model of equality in importance, honor, and respect, while maintaining differentness in roles and functions within the family was the universal model for the Christian family. Theologians call this the "order of creation." This expression shows that this union between husband and wife was established by God already in the Garden of Eden between Adam and Eve. It is not the result of the fall into sin. This model has always been part and parcel of what it means to be male and female within marriage.

Colossae had a very similar context to Corinth and Ephesus. It was about 120 miles east of Ephesus. It, too, was part of the Roman Empire and had roots in ancient Greece. Epaphras is named in Colossians 1:7 as the one who taught them about Christ and who therefore probably also founded the congregation there. As new Christian converts, the members of the Church in Colossae had to rethink everything they had been taught about god, life, and ethics. The verses cited above are part of a larger discussion about the nature of Jesus' saving love. If one were to read them in isolation from the rest of Colossians, they sound like snippets of old Jewish law: "wives submit to your husbands," "husbands love your wives," "children obey your parents," "fathers do not be mean to your children." But when the larger context of Colossians is considered, these snippets take on a different character. They become the natural outward expressions of the love of Christ.

The Colossians, like other idol worshippers in the Roman Empire, were taught that their gods each carved out their own little niches. One god was said to be concerned with crops, another with weather, and another with war. Each god had his or her own special realm. What one wanted to accomplish determined to which god one needed to pray or make offerings. The gods were limited, compartmentalized, and each affected only one small aspect of a person's life. Christianity was different. In Colossae, St. Paul focused on Jesus as encompassing everything. He filled all creation, and He filled every aspect of daily life.

> For by him all things were created, in heaven and on earth, visible and invisible, whether thrones or dominions or rulers or authorities—all things were created through him and for him. And he is before all things, and in him all things hold together. And he is the head of the body, the church. He is the beginning, the firstborn from the dead, that in everything he might be preeminent. For in him all the fullness of God was pleased to dwell, and through him to reconcile to himself all things, whether on earth or in heaven, making peace by the blood of his cross. And you, who once were alienated and hostile in mind, doing evil deeds, he has now reconciled in his body of

flesh by his death, in order to present you holy and blameless and above reproach before him. (Colossians 1:16–22)

Jesus as One who encompasses everything in creation and everything about the individual, naturally, would encompass the relations of people with each other, including that of husband and wife, parents and children. Paul was very brief in what he said about these relationships, but he was consistent with what he said elsewhere. The submission of the wife to the husband is not a legalistic command; instead, it is defined by the broader saving work of Christ "as is fitting [or as is proper] in the Lord." Being included in the all-encompassing love of Christ had an effect on the relational role of wife to husband and husband to wife. Christ defined the heart and mind of each toward the other. Both husband and wife were equally remade through grace into new beings possessing new purer interactions with each other.

Paul's mention of husband and wife in verses 18 and 19 follows his discussion of the new life placed into all Christians just a few verses earlier.

> Set your minds on things that are above, not on things that are on earth. For you have died, and your life is hidden with Christ in God. When Christ who is your life appears, then you also will appear with him in glory. Put to death therefore what is earthly in you: sexual immorality, impurity, passion, evil desire, and covetousness, which is idolatry. On account of these the wrath of God is coming. In these you too once walked, when you were living in them. But now you must put them all away: anger, wrath, malice, slander, and obscene talk from your mouth. Do not lie to one another, seeing that you have put off the old self with its practices and have put on the new self, which is being renewed in knowledge after the image of its creator. Here there is not Greek and Jew, circumcised and uncircumcised, barbarian, Scythian, slave, free; but Christ is all, and in all. (Colossians 3:2–11)

Being joined to Christ meant that older pagan notions of sexual conduct were undone. One could not reflect Christ properly if one was still "sexually immoral, impure, or given to adulterous passions and evil desires." Those who "put on the new self" put on the life of Christ with His chastity and His self-control. This would have been, and in fact still is, a radical way of understanding sexual morality. Paul's Christian ethic is not based primarily on laws decreed by God to ancient Israel. Christian morality is based on Christ's all-encompassing purity and self-emptying love. It is not just what Christians are to do; it is who they now are in Christ. They are changed at their core, so they live in new ways. Christians could no longer live as Greeks or Romans. Their worldview and self-view was distinctly different. They were now one with Christ in heart and soul.

To the rest of the world around them, this Christian morality was contrary to the basic ideals of society. Paul makes no apologies for putting these newly converted Christians at odds with the world around them. Yes, they would feel the disapproval of the world in which they lived. It would cause some uncomfortable moments with family and friends. In some cases, it might even get them murdered under the excuse of sparing society from their twisted views. Paul knew, as did his newly converted brothers and sisters, that the love of Christ would not spare them from suffering; it would *invite* suffering. But they could face society's rejection because the hatred of the world was overcome by the love of Christ. He would deliver them from the world and set them into God's eternal glory.

1 Peter 3:1, 7

> Likewise, wives, be subject to your own husbands, so that even
> if some do not obey the word, they may be won without a word
> by the conduct of their wives. . . . Likewise, husbands, live with
> your wives in an understanding way, showing honor to the
> woman as the weaker vessel, since they are heirs with you of
> the grace of life, so that your prayers may not be hindered.

I have included these verses from 1 Peter to show consistency of thought between the apostles. It is believed that St. Peter wrote this epistle from Rome shortly before he was executed under the persecution of Christians begun by Nero. His audience seems to be both Jewish and Gentile converts scattered over a large area. He states in the first verse of this epistle, "To those who are elect exiles of the Dispersion in Pontus, Galatia, Cappadocia, Asia, and Bithynia." The broadness of his intended audience and the fact that his teachings echo those of Paul on the relation of husband and wife show that these principles for marriage were universal. They were to apply to all Christians.

Peter, like Paul, emphasized ideas of subjection for Christian wives to their husbands. He showed that these principles are part of a greater apostolic teaching and not just limited to Paul. This subjection or yielding to the other is a disposition meant to show forth Christ. God works through such subjection, because, as Peter explains, wives who show such deference to their husbands bear witness to Christ and become vehicles for the Holy Spirit to convert unbelieving husbands.

The woman is not lesser than the man because she is subject to him. She bears a unique and powerful witness of Christian love in her vocation as wife. She is further defined as an "heir with you of the grace of life." Both husband and wife are equal heirs of God's saving grace. Both are equally loved, redeemed, and sanctified. Their roles are different, but their value is equal, and this is not taught through force of laws dictating behaviors, but through the Gospel, which redefines individuals in relation to Christ and each other.

What some today would label as demeaning of women, namely their role as wives subject to the love of their husbands, the early Christian converts understood as an elevation of womanhood. Woman was granted an equality of purpose and value in the eyes of God. It may be because of the high regard for womanhood that many of the early converts among Romans were women. One of the accusations made against Christianity by the Romans was that Christianity only attracted women and uneducated people.[11] There is truth in the accusation that Christianity afforded a sense of dignity and importance to those whom Roman society oppressed. Women who were used to being treated poorly found in Christ a status of love and respect not found in the state religion.

sexual morality and homosexual sex

The Gospel of Christ is not concerned only with the immaterial soul or life after death. Christianity seeks the redemption of the flesh. God became flesh in the person of Jesus. Jesus was killed in His flesh and rose

---

[11] Alexander Roberts, Sir James Donaldson, and Arthur Cleveland Cox, ed., "Fathers of the Third Century," in *The Ante-Nicene Fathers* vol. IV (New York: Cosimo Inc., 2007), 177. A quote from the antagonist in Minucius Felix *"Octavius, VIII,"* which is aimed against Christians, reads, "Having gathered together from the lowest dregs the more unskilled, and women, credulous and, by the facility of their sex, yielding, establish a herd of a profane conspiracy, which is leagued together by nightly meetings, and solemn fasts and inhuman meats."

from the dead in the flesh. He is now ascended into heaven according to His flesh. He promises that His fleshly resurrection will one day mean our fleshly resurrection. And perhaps even more shocking for Roman ears that were used to thinking of their gods as dwelling off in a distant mountain or being found in the temples they built for them, the God of Christianity claims our human flesh as His dwelling place. Paul tells the Corinthians,

> Do you not know that your body is a temple of the Holy Spirit within you, whom you have from God? You are not your own, for you were bought with a price. So glorify God in your body. (1 Corinthians 6:19–20)

The God preached by St. Paul actually joins Himself to the flesh of the people who believe in Him. Faith represents a change of ownership with our flesh. Our bodies are no longer ours to do with as we please. Jesus paid for our bodies by sacrificing His own. Because our flesh is God's dwelling place and He owns it through the purchase price of His Son, God shows the world something of His purity and love through our flesh. This is the heart of Christian ethics and morality. It is not an ethics bound exclusively to laws. We do not live as we do just because the Bible says we have to. Christian ethics grow from the Gospel. We live as we do because God has made us His own. He joined Himself to us. He bought us by giving up His Son's life for us. Paul's ethic of sexual chastity is a natural extension of an overall ethic of changed being. We live differently than the world around us because God changed us when He joined Himself to our flesh. His purity manifests itself in us through all our relationships. Sexual chastity is only one aspect of the new divine holiness that dwells in us.

This is not to say that Law does not enter into questions of sexual ethics. We should not need the Law to tell us what is and is not godly because God does dwell within us and we are purchased through Jesus' self-emptying sacrifice. Yet sin does continue to stick to us. Martin Luther used to say that we are simultaneously saint and sinner. Because we continually transgress the holiness that God gives us, we need the Law. Paul recognized this. As he taught about sexual ethics, he applied both Law and Gospel to the issue.

The following pages will show Paul employing both Law and Gospel to the problem of immorality. It should be noticed that Paul does not treat homosexual sins differently than heterosexual sins when it comes to the application of Law and Gospel. Both are addressed side by side as equally contrary to God's Law and both are spoken of as equally forgivable. There are only rare instances where Paul singles out homosexual sins for special mention (as in Romans 1). This is an important lesson for modern Christians. We can fall into the trap of false piety, where we become very offended at homosexual sins but cast only a brief frown at heterosexual sins. If we hear some young man had intercourse with a young woman, we may voice our displeasure, but we might also be quick to embrace him back into our good graces once we hear he is sorry. We probably will not treat him differently going forward. Things can be very different if we hear of a young man who had sexual contact with another young man. We might treat him differently going forward. Out of false piety, we might ostracize him and turn away from him with such righteous disgust that it becomes impossible to continue with the same relationship as before. We Christians can be guilty at times of operating with a double standard when it comes to sexual sins. What St. Paul shows us is an equal treatment for all sexual sins. There is not an extra level of disgust when it comes to homosexual sins. All sexual sins demand repentance and all can be forgiven.

1 CORINTHIANS 6:9-11

> Or do you not know that the unrighteous will not inherit the kingdom of God? Do not be deceived: neither the sexually immoral, nor idolaters, nor adulterers, nor men who practice homosexuality, nor thieves, nor the greedy, nor drunkards, nor revilers, nor swindlers will inherit the kingdom of God. And such were some of you. But you were washed, you were sanctified, you were justified in the name of the Lord Jesus Christ and by the Spirit of our God.

This passage is especially important in understanding the transformative power of grace and the permeating power of sin. Both sin and grace become matters of self-identification. Sin is not merely something one does or a blemish that can be ignored if the rest of the person is well-groomed. As Paul speaks of it, sin defines the individual before God. He lists ten sins and concludes the list by saying, "Such were some of you." It is not that the people merely did those things; they were those things. Sin defined the individual without Christ.

What is especially meaningful, however, is what the grace and forgiveness of Christ does to those defined by their sins. Paul says, "Such *were* some of you." The reconciling power of Christ does more than wash away the past bad things we do from God's memory, it redefines who we are. "But you were washed, you were sanctified, you were justified in the name of the Lord Jesus Christ and by the Spirit of our God." Grace changes us at the core.

This is an important issue for those who may identify as homosexual but who know and believe that homosexuality is contrary to God's will. They may be repentant of their same-sex attractions and want to be rid of them but are unable to change by simply willing it. It can be helpful for them to understand that in Christ, the redeemed have a new self-identification. They are not homosexual, though they may be tempted by homosexual sins. Sin no longer defines them, but it does continue to harass them. In Christ, they are washed (baptized),[12] sanctified (marked with the holiness of God's Spirit), and justified (forgiven and reconciled to God). These are the things that now define who they are to (and in) Christ.

The meaning of the words in these passages is often made a point of debate. To support their premise, people use definitions of words that are not always honest to the context in which they are found. They will challenge long-standing meanings by claiming that the Greek allows for alternate meanings. Since the average person does not generally know Greek, it can be difficult to counter these arguments. Because of this, I will cite the Greek words involved and offer some background to those words so those unfamiliar with Greek can better understand Paul's use of them.

The first two words Paul uses in this passage address heterosexual sins. We have reviewed them already above. The "sexually immoral" is the Greek word *pornoi* (πόρνοι). Although it was originally a word having to do with prostitution, by Paul's day it held a much broader meaning. As Paul uses the word here, it is a broad condemnation against any sexual immorality, which means any sexual activity outside marriage. The next word Paul uses is *moichoi* (μοιχοι = adulterers). It is the noun form of the verb *moichao* that was discussed earlier in this chapter. Primarily (though not exclusively), it deals with those who are unfaithful to their spouses.

---

[12] Lockwood, *1 Corinthians*, 202. As Lockwood points out, the Greek word λουτρῷ (*loutro*), "to wash" is a word commonly used in connection with Baptism in the New Testament.

Unfaithfulness need not be a sexual act. Jesus used the verb form of this word to include those who looked lustfully at women.

It is worth noting that as Paul lists the sexual sins that define people, heterosexual sins are first on his list. They are placed conspicuously on either side of the word *idolatry*. This in itself says something. Sexual sins were and are sins of idolatry inasmuch as one puts his or her own fleshly desires ahead of God's will and makes the human will superior to that of God. The self becomes an idol. It is also worth noting that heterosexual sins are named first and condemned more often than homosexual sins. This becomes all the more important when we understand the great prevalence of homosexuality in ancient Rome. It is not that Paul was just naïve and did not really know how much homosexuality was around him. Paul knew how accepted it was and chose to address heterosexual sins more often.

The ESV combines two separate Greek words for "homosexual" into the phrase, "Men who practice homosexuality." This is unfortunate, because the two words mean slightly different things. The first Greek word is *malakoi* (μαλαϰοὶ). This is the word discussed previously that literally means "soft ones." Here it should be understood in light of the Roman mind. It was an insult to call an adult man "soft" in Roman culture. In terms of sexual behavior, *malakos* connoted a male who played the female in intercourse or the one who passively allowed himself to be sodomized by another male. The second Greek word is "sodomites" (*arsenokoitai*, ἀρσενοϰοῖται). This is a compound word made of *arsen* (ἄρσην), which means "male," and *koitae* (ϰοίτη), a word whose primary meaning is "bed" but euphemistically means "intercourse." It is the equivalent of the English word *coitus*. The compound word means "male-sex."[13] This word addresses the other side of homosexual intercourse and describes the one who is actively doing the sodomizing. Paul includes both elements of homosexual behavior in his condemnation. Those who are penetrated by another and those doing the penetrating are both listed. Paul could not be any more descriptive of the problem he was addressing.

To summarize the importance of this passage from 1 Corinthians 6,

1. It clearly treats all forms of adultery and of homosexual behavior as categories of sexual sin.

---

[13] BDAG, 135. "One who has intercourse with a man as with a woman, a male who engages in sexual activity with a person of his own sex."

2. It groups these sins together with other sins like stealing, idolatry, and drunkenness, making them all equally serious.

3. As this passage is used in the debate about homosexuality, it leaves no doubt that both the active and passive partners in homosexual relationships are acting contrary to God's will.

4. There is no exception given to make homosexuality not sinful, for instance, if the couple is in a "loving relationship"; just as there is no exception given for heterosexual intercourse outside of marriage. Any sexual activity that is not between a man and woman bound together in marriage is sin.

5. Perhaps most important, all sins listed are treated as equally forgivable, and those caught in them are described as a people who can be changed by God. "Such *were* some of you. But you were washed, you were sanctified, you were justified in the name of the Lord Jesus Christ and by the Spirit of our God."

Contrary to what some believe, homosexual sins can be repented of, turned away from, and forgiven the same as heterosexual sins. As Paul discusses sexual sins, including homosexuality, he states, "Such were some of you." His use of the past tense "were" is indicative of a substantial change, not just in behavior but in one's identity. Those previously named as homosexuals were redefined by Christ through repentance so that they are no longer homosexuals. Homosexual sin is not an unforgiveable sin, nor are those caught in it incapable of change. We will speak more on this in a later chapter.

Romans 1

For his invisible attributes, namely, his eternal power and divine nature, have been clearly perceived, ever since the creation of the world, in the things that have been made. So they are without excuse. For although they knew God, they did not honor him as God or give thanks to him, but they became futile in their thinking, and their foolish hearts were darkened. Claiming to be wise, they became fools, and exchanged the glory of the immortal God for images resembling mortal man and birds and animals and creeping things. Therefore God gave them up in the lusts of their hearts to impurity, to the dishonoring of their bodies among themselves, because they exchanged the truth about God for a lie and worshiped and served the creature rather than the Creator, who is blessed forever! Amen.

For this reason God gave them up to dishonorable passions. For their women exchanged natural relations for those that are contrary to nature; and the men likewise gave up natural relations with women and were consumed with passion for one another, men committing shameless acts with men and receiving in themselves the due penalty for their error.

And since they did not see fit to acknowledge God, God gave them up to a debased mind to do what ought not to be done. (Romans 1:20–28)

This is the only text in the Bible that explicitly addresses both male and female homosexual sins. Where 1 Corinthians 6:9 connected the sin of idolatry to heterosexual sins by sandwiching it between adultery and immorality, Romans 1 links idolatry to homosexual sins. As St. Paul explains it, "They exchanged the truth about God for a lie and worshiped and served the creature rather than the Creator. For this reason God gave them up to dishonorable passions." Paul links the sexual immorality of Rome, singling out homosexual acts, to the broader sin of idolatry. Rome's worship of its gods did shape how people understood relations with each other, socially and sexually.

The Roman Context Revisited

In Rome, there were temples and shrines built to hundreds of gods. Caesar Augustus, the Caesar in power when Jesus was born, was especially fond of the god Apollo. He built a huge statue of Apollo with his private residence nearby.[14] Other popular deities in Rome included Jupiter, Juno, Venus, Mars, Mercury, Vulcan, Cupid, Bacchus, and Vesta. Each occupation and vocation had special gods or goddesses who were thought to give blessings to their unique needs. There were also household spirits, gods, and ancestors worshiped by the common citizens. As said before, the Caesars were deified and worshiped as gods. Caesar Augustus claimed to be descended from the gods Venus and Mars.

---

[14] Henry Boren, *Roman Society*, 2nd ed. (Lexington, MA: D. C. Heath and Co. 1992), 168.

Augustus referred to himself as *divi filius* (son of god), a title for Caesar that was stamped on the common Roman denarius.

The Roman myths about their gods were filled with stories of adultery, incest, and homosexuality. For example, in Greek/Roman mythology, the god Zeus (Jupiter) took Juno (Hera), his sister, to be his wife (coincidently Zeus's father Cronus was also married to his sister, Rhea). He had four children with her (Vulcan, Mars, Juventas, and Lucina). Zeus cheated on Juno and loved the goddess Metis, fathering the goddess Athena by her. He also loved Leto, daughter of two Titans, and from her had Apollo and Artemis. By a mortal woman named Alcmene, he fathered Hercules. Zeus assumed the form of her husband who was away in battle to satisfy his lust for her. From the Spartan queen Leda, he fathered two sets of twins. To impregnate her, he assumed the form of a swan. He took Ganymede, a Trojan prince, as a homosexual lover assuming the form of an eagle. He seduced a Phoenician princess named Europa in the form of a white bull. He impregnated the mortal woman Io whom he turned into a white heifer to hide her from his jealous wife, Hera. He impregnated Danae, a princess, through the form of a shower of gold. Perseus was the son resulting from that union. There are more stories of other adulterous acts of Zeus with various women and goddesses. Zeus as the king of the gods was thought to be the supreme example of the divine will. According to their mythology, he was the ultimate authority for upholding law and morality among the gods. If the keeper of law and morality is himself immoral, the ethic taught by such stories cannot help but promote immorality and disrespect for marriage and women among the common people.

The stories of the gods contributed a great deal to the formation of Rome's self-definition. Roman religion was woven into the fabric of everyday life. There was not a public event where the gods were not invoked. Major political decisions were usually preceded by consultation with oracles and offerings to certain gods. Sporting events began with ceremonies to one or more of the gods. Christians refused to participate in the worship of the Roman gods. Their refusal became a very noticeable public protest.[15] The Romans interpreted the Christians' public refusals to worship their gods as attacks on Roman society, and indeed, as attacks on humanity in general. The following excerpt from Tacitus' *Annals*

---

[15] Boren, *Roman Society*, 290, 294.

shows the Roman mindset toward Christians. Tacitus was a Roman senator and historian born during the reign of Nero.

> Consequently, to get rid of the report [*that Nero himself ordered the fire that burned Rome*], Nero fastened the guilt and inflicted the most exquisite tortures on a class hated for their abominations, called Christians by the populace. Christus, from whom the name had its origin, suffered the extreme penalty during the reign of Tiberius at the hands of one of our procurators, Pontius Pilatus, and a most mischievous superstition, thus checked for the moment, again broke out not only in Judaea, the first source of the evil, but even in Rome, where all things hideous and shameful from every part of the world find their center and become popular. Accordingly, an arrest was first made of all who pleaded guilty; then, upon their information, an immense multitude was convicted, not so much of the crime of firing the city, as of hatred against mankind. Mockery of every sort was added to their deaths. Covered with the skins of beasts, they were torn by dogs and perished, or were nailed to crosses, or were doomed to the flames and burnt, to serve as a nightly illumination, when daylight had expired.[16]

From Tacitus we learn that the Romans thought the Christians guilty of "abominations." Claims against Christians included cannibalism, because Christians claimed to eat the body of Christ and drink His blood. The charge of "hatred against mankind" undoubtedly stemmed from the Christian refusal to participate in the normal rites and ceremonies of Roman citizens who offered devotion to the many gods of Rome. This was seen as an attack against the eternal hopes of the rest of humanity. Misunderstanding of Christian rites and beliefs do not explain all of the charges made against Christians. Outright lies were aimed at Christians to make them the most hated people on earth. Christians were accused of tearing babies to pieces and eating their flesh. The accusation of incest was made repeatedly against Christians.[17]

---

[16] Cornelius Tacitus, *Annals of Tacitus*, 304–305. Italics added.

[17] Beard, North, and Price, *Religions of Rome*, vol. 2 (Cambridge: Cambridge University Press, 1998), 280–281.

back to the passage

It is in this context of idolatry and viscous hatred of Christianity that we must understand Paul's words to the Romans. As he addressed the homosexuality prevalent in Rome of which the Caesars and Nero especially were guilty, he began by discussing the idolatrous mindset behind it. And while he here singles out homosexuality, it is fair to say that all immoral sexual practices and objectification of people could be tied to Rome's fundamental religious beliefs.

Idolatry is at the heart of all immorality and, one could argue, precedes it. In the Old Testament, when God accused the Israelites of idolatry, He called them adulterers. Through the prophet Ezekiel, God expresses sorrow over Israel, "Then those of you who escape will remember me among the nations where they are carried captive, how I have been broken over their whoring heart that has departed from me and over their eyes that go whoring after their idols. And they will be loathsome in their own sight for the evils that they have committed, for all their abominations" (Ezekiel 6:9). God's people lavished the love they were supposed to show exclusively to Him on false gods instead. Worship is an expression of love. God, who has shown the infinite depth of His love to us in sending His Son to be the sacrifice for our sins, expects that we will love Him above everything else. "Hear, O Israel: The LORD our God, the LORD is one. You shall love the LORD your God with all your heart and with all your soul and with all your might" (Deuteronomy 6:4–5). To engage in the worship of anyone or anything other than the one true God is to break a holy bond of love sealed in the blood of God's own Son. Therefore, idolatry offends against love and is linked to all other offenses against love, like homosexuality and other acts of immorality.

romans 1 and temple prostitution

There are those within the homosexual community who have tried to build a case from Rome's idolatry, claiming that Romans 1 is only talking about that form of homosexuality associated with the worship of certain gods and goddesses, like Cybele, who was worshiped through temple prostitution. The claim is made that in Cybele's temple, castrated male priests would give themselves to be sodomized by male worshippers. That, and *only that*, is what Paul was condemning in Romans 1.

There are several problems with this view. First, Paul simply does not say that his focus was only on temple prostitution. He certainly does not single out the goddess Cybele. On the contrary, when Paul describes the nature of the idolatry that he was condemning, he speaks of the many false gods of Rome without distinction.

> Claiming to be wise, they became fools, and exchanged the glory of the immortal God for images resembling mortal man and birds and animals and creeping things. Therefore God gave them up in the lusts of their hearts to impurity, to the dishonoring of their bodies among themselves, because they exchanged the truth about God for a lie and worshiped and served the creature rather than the Creator, who is blessed forever! Amen.

Paul's eye is on the sum total of the idolatry of Rome and its effect on the people who worshiped false gods. Their love for the created things over the Creator led them to dishonor their bodies among themselves. Again, Paul does not limit this "dishonoring of their bodies" to ritualistic sex within certain temples. He is speaking of a general dishonoring seen throughout Roman culture, exemplified by the idolatrous mythology of the Romans that was permeated with stories of immorality and homosexual activity. The Roman people justified their immorality and engaged in homosexual practices with support from the example of their gods. This included temple prostitution, but it certainly was not limited to specific temple practices. Paul was scholarly enough that if he had in mind only the specific case of temple prostitution, he would have made his point clearly.

Another problem with this limited understanding of Romans 1 is that this is not the only passage where Paul condemns homosexual sin. Romans 1 must be seen in light of all the other passages discussed in this chapter. Paul is very clear that any form of homosexuality is contrary to God. Romans 1 forms one small discussion in a much broader conversation about sexual chastity and immorality. Together, the whole of these New Testament witnesses shows that there is only one God-pleasing expression for sex, and that is between a man and a woman who are bound together in marriage.

god gave them up

"For this reason God gave them up to dishonorable passions." "For this reason," that is, for the reason of pervasive idolatry and love of false gods "God gave them up to vile passions." The Greek word most versions of the Bible translate as "gave up" is *paredoken* (παρέδωκεν). This is the past tense of the verb *paradidomi* (παραδίδωμι) that literally means "to hand over, or give over"; such as when one might give a prisoner over into the custody of another. In the standard scholarly Greek English Lexicon (Bauer, Danker, Arndt, and Gingrich), this word in the context of Romans 1 is said to carry the idea that God "abandoned them" to impurity.[18] God turned them over to the custody of their false gods to do those things which their false beliefs dictated and their false gods modeled.

The idea of "God giving someone up" or "abandoning them" is a very difficult idea with which to come to terms. We normally speak of God's willingness to forgive any and all sins. In the 1 Corinthians 6 passage reviewed earlier, Paul spoke of people who were sexually immoral, and he included in his list those who were homosexual and those who were promiscuous heterosexuals. But then Paul said, "Such were some of you," which shows that there was forgiveness and restoration for those guilty of such sins. Here, however, the message is harsher. He uses the word *paredoken* (παρέδωκεν) three times in this reading (vv. 24, 26, and 28) to stress the fact that God had actively changed His heart toward them as a consequence of their hardened impenitence toward Him. Why the difference? The same sin is listed in both passages. The difference lies not in the nature of the sin committed, but in the nature of the people of whom Paul was speaking. In 1 Corinthians 6, Paul was talking to Gentile converts who had received Christ, repented of their former idolatry and sin, and were now baptized Christians. In Romans, Paul was talking about Roman society, which continued to reject Christ and His message of restoration to God. He was talking about people who were still wholly given over to the idolatry of Rome.[19]

Christian theology does acknowledge the biblical reality of God hardening the hearts of the unrepentant. He hardened Pharaoh's heart in Exodus for refusing God's call to let His people go. Initially, Pharaoh hardened his own heart against God (Exodus 8:15, 32), but eventually

---

[18] BDAG, 762.

[19] Cf. Michael Middendorf, *Concordia Commentary: Romans 1–8* (St. Louis: Concordia, 2013), 113. Middendorf shows that the threefold "giving over" of God is preceded by a threefold "exchanging" of God's truth for sin. People exchanged the glory of God for idol worship, God's truth for the lie, and natural sexual relations for homosexual activity. God's giving them over was a response to their persistent giving up on God.

God hardened Pharaoh's heart (Exodus 9:12). God "gave him up" to his own unbelief. On those rare occasions when the Bible mentions God hardening the heart of some individual, it is always preceded by the individual hardening his or her heart against God. God's active hardening of the sinner's heart only confirms what the individual first chose to do against God. It is by sheer grace and compassion from God that we are not all hardened because of our disobedience.

A hardened heart is one that will not change or be persuaded otherwise. God can see whose hearts are truly hardened and whose are not. We, on the other hand, cannot see hardening of hearts and must assume that the person before us can be reached by Christ and brought to repentance. Repentance can be extremely difficult for those caught in sexual sins (heterosexual or homosexual). Some people may come to see their behaviors as part of their self-identification to the point that it becomes nearly impossible for them to imagine themselves any differently. They may, as in Rome, surrender to their urges and accept their sin as natural.

I once had a senior pastor with nearly forty years of parish experience tell me that of all the people he counseled over the years, the one group of sins that he had never seen anyone completely break free from, and he stressed "anyone," was sexual sins. Sex does trigger very powerful chemical reactions in the brain that can and do become addicting. Sexual addiction is a recognized psychological/physical malady. Any form of improper sexual activity can become the drug of choice in a sexual addiction. In Rome, when St. Paul says that God gave those engaged in homosexual practices over to a debased mind, he may very well have been identifying what we now know to be medically true. People's brain chemistry can become dependent on unhealthy, sinful, sexual practices to the point where their flesh craves sex like an addict craves his or her next fix.

During my twenty-five years of ministry, I have personally dealt with people struggling with both homosexual and heterosexual sins. The symptoms they exhibit follow the pattern of physical/psychological addiction. They ignore the signs of destruction piling up around them. They are willing to suffer the loss of public image, finances, friends, family, and even their own health to continue their behavior. They understand their behavior is causing spiritual problems and ruining their life with Christ, but they will not stop. They may say they want to change, but somehow just cannot. Such is the nature of addiction.

What Paul describes in Romans as the spiritual state of being "given up" by God may reflect the reality of a person hardened in unrepentance and addicted to aberrant behavior. This does not mean that all addictions are examples of being "given up" by God. Addictions of any kind can be broken, but it is a hard, painful journey. Paul applies the expression of being "given up" to the Roman situation and those given over to idols. This is not a blanket statement that can be applied to all those guilty of homosexual sins. First Corinthians 6 is clear that repentance and turning away from homosexual sins is possible, same as any other sin. But Paul's words in Romans 1 should stand as a warning to all who would choose to engage in sexual immorality. Sexual sins can create dependence issues leading to unrepentance and ultimately to being hardened in one's heart and given up by God.

romans 1 and sins against nature

Paul introduces another argument against the homosexual practices in Romans 1 that goes beyond the issue of idolatry. In verses 26 and following, Paul talks about women and men abandoning "the natural use" of the other sex for what is "against nature." The idea that homosexuality is a sin against nature is a point of heated debate. The pro-homosexual community champions the idea that homosexuality is as natural as heterosexuality. Volumes have been written claiming homosexuality is found throughout the animal kingdom.[20] Because there are examples of same-sex animals copulating, the argument is made that homosexuality is "natural," even "normal" throughout the animal kingdom. During my lectures, students were fond of pointing to examples of monkeys and dolphins, which are known to display homosexual behavior regularly (males among males). Their conclusion was that Paul did not know what he was talking about and made an argument that can be proven false.

In answer to their complaints, I pointed out that the sexual behavior of animals cannot be equated to that of humans. God's Word teaches that mankind is made in the image of God; animals are not. God has endowed humanity with a sense of right and wrong that He has not given to the animals. They act on urges that are alien to us as humans and that our sense of morality would prohibit. For example, "Why do animals have sexual intercourse?" Obviously, they have intercourse for the sake of

---

[20] For example, Bruce Bagemihl, *Biological Exuberance: Animal Homosexuality and Natural Diversity* (New York: St. Martin's Press, 1999). This volume contains many pictures and examples of mostly male animals copulating with other male animals, to prove homosexuality is natural.

procreation, but they also use sexual contact as a statement of dominance and a means of social control. Studies of certain monkeys have shown how a dominant male will use intercourse (on both female and male monkeys) to control social unrest. When such behavior is practiced by people, we call it rape. Rape is essentially an expression of dominance over another person. It is more an act of violence than sex. What may come naturally to certain animals cannot be used to justify human behavior. Additionally, what animals, especially male animals, exhibit is not "homosexual" in the sense that they are exclusively attracted to male animals. Animals that use sexual contact to establish dominance and social control copulate with both males and females, exhibiting bisexual, not homosexual, behavior.

Furthermore, animal sexuality is driven by forces beyond the human experience. Scent and pheromones trigger sexual responses in animals that they cannot control. Cows are known to mount each other when in heat. They are not trying to have sex with each other, but their behavior has been interpreted by some as representing a homosexual act. A dog latching on the leg of one person but not another is hardly driven by any sense of love or attraction understandable on a human level. Every autumn when I trudge into the woods to hunt deer, I watch does run past me in fear as they are being chased by bucks. This past year, I witnessed a buck so exhausted from chasing does that his tongue was hanging out and he was frothing at the mouth and panting deeply; he looked like he could drop at any moment. During such a rut, bucks lose their "rational" mind and pursue behaviors that are self-destructive. The point being, sexual behavior in animals is not the same as human behavior. It is driven by forces alien to human sexuality, and it is wrong to interpret animal sexual behaviors as natural expressions for human behavior.

Paul's point about intercourse that is contrary to nature can be made quite simply by appealing to anatomy. Nature is brutally simple. Every orifice of the body is designed for a specific natural purpose. When it comes to those organs used for sexual activity, there are orifices designed to be entrances and those designed to be exits. The anus is not naturally designed to be an entry point into the human body. It is well documented within the medical profession that anal sex leads to a high rate of anal trauma—such as rips, tears, and abrasions—because people try to force their bodies to do what they were not designed to do. It is also well-known that anal intercourse leads to a greater rate of transmitted disease than vaginal intercourse. Pathogens pass through the walls of the colon much easier than through the vaginal wall. Oral sexual activity leads to the direct ingestion of those materials most likely to carry diseases and parasites. Upsetting the natural design of the human body and using the sexual organs in ways contrary to the clear intent of the Creator makes for problems.

The one constant rule of nature is that the continuation of a species requires males and females to mate. Paul is correct when he says that homosexual activity goes against nature, inasmuch as there would be no propagation of species without heterosexual activity. The argument that examples of homosexual behavior in the animal kingdom prove that homosexuality is natural is not universally accepted by advocates of the homosexual lifestyle. Noted feminist author, professor, and self-professed lesbian, Camille Paglia stated:

> Homosexuality is not "normal." On the contrary it is a challenge to the norm; Nature exists whether academics like it or not. And in nature, procreation is the single relentless rule. That is the norm. Our sexual bodies were designed for reproduction. Penis fits vagina: no fancy linguistic game-playing can change that biologic fact.[21]

Paul's argument from nature is sound. The human sexual organs are designed for sexual activity leading to procreation. Males and females are designed to complete each other. In the language of the Old Testament, they are designed to become one flesh. In fact, every other organ of the human body completes its function in itself without the necessity of the opposite sex. Hearts beat, stomachs digest, eyes see at full efficiency within individuals. But the sexual organs require a member of the opposite sex to complete the function for which they were designed, namely procreation. Whether or not children are conceived from that union is beside the point. The organs of the human body as male and female were created to fit together for that function. This is the meaning of Paul's argument involving "natural use" versus "what is against nature."

1 Timothy 1:8-11

> Now we know that the law is good, if one uses it lawfully, understanding this, that the law is not laid down for the just but

---

[21] Camille Paglia, *Vamps and Tramps* (New York: Vintage Books, 1994), 70–71.

for the lawless and disobedient, for the ungodly and sinners, for the unholy and profane, for those who strike their fathers and mothers, for murderers, the sexually immoral, men who practice homosexuality, enslavers, liars, perjurers, and whatever else is contrary to sound doctrine, in accordance with the gospel of the glory of the blessed God with which I have been entrusted.

Paul uses many of the same terms here that he used in 1 Corinthians 6. The term *sexually immoral* is the Greek word *pornois* (πόρνοις), which is used as a general term for those whose sexual activity is not within the marriage bond of husband and wife. The Greek term used here for "men who practice homosexuality" is *arsenokoitais* (ἀρσενοκοίταις), the compound word meaning "male-coitus." The placement of these words within a list of things "contrary to sound doctrine" shows how antithetical such practices are to the Christian faith. To practice any of the sins listed is to be "lawless and disobedient" in the eyes of God. Homosexuality is given equal treatment with heterosexual immorality as aberrant behavior, which if not repented of, will separate one from God.

Contrary to popular accusations, Christian opposition to homosexuality is in no way based on hatred of homosexuals. The Bible is equally firm that heterosexual intercourse outside the estate of marriage is wrong; no one suggests that the prohibition against heterosexual immorality is born out of hatred for heterosexuals. This passage is yet another voice in a much larger chorus stressing the same basic message: there is only one God-given context for proper sexual expression, namely, heterosexual marriage. Any sexual contact between unmarried persons or between people of the same sex, any sexual desire in the form of lust for another person, is contrary to God's will in the same way that those "who strike their fathers and mothers, murderers, the sexually immoral, men who practice homosexuality, enslavers, liars, and perjurers" act contrary to sound doctrine.

general passages on sexual conduct

How a person conducts him or herself sexually does affect that person's relationship to God. The Bible is full of passages that make this case. To foster a better understanding of what these passages say, I have placed the Greek word being translated next to the English. In the following passages there are four Greek words used repeatedly. *Porneia* (πορνεία) was discussed above; it is a word that originally had to do with prostitution but eventually took on the general meaning of "sexual immorality." *Moicheia* (μοιχεία) refers to adultery or sexual acts with someone who is not one's spouse. *Akatharsia* (ἀκαθαρσία) means "1. any substance that is filthy or dirty, *refuse*. 2. a state of moral corruption."[22] It is a more general term that has several uses. When used for immorality, it takes on a similar meaning to the English word *dirty*. It may be found with *porneia*, as a further descriptor of sexual impurity or in connection to the uncleanness of idolatry. Its most common use is in connection with demons as an adjective, i.e., "unclean spirits." In every context and with every meaning, though, the basic thought is that it is contrary to the purity of God. *Aselgeia* (ἀσέλγεια) is a term for sexual excess. It carries the meaning of licentiousness or debauchery or lacking moral restraint.[23]

These words for sexual sins are found throughout the Bible and are aimed at both Jews and Gentiles. Their use across a broad spectrum of audiences shows that they are to be applied to all people. Our goal with presenting these passages is not to dissect them verse by verse but to offer all together as a sort of *tour de force* to demonstrate the consistency of Scripture. These words convey divine moral truth meant to be applicable to all times and all cultures. They do not mince words about the seriousness of sexual sins. They are condemnatory and clear and make obvious to anyone reading them that a Savior is needed to rescue us, because all stand guilty of what they say.

> **Matthew 15:19–20a**—For out of the heart come evil thoughts, murder, adultery (*moicheia*), sexual immorality (*porneia*), theft, false witness, slander. These are what defile a person.

> **2 Corinthians 12:21**—I fear that when I come again my God may humble me before you, and I may have to mourn over many of those who sinned earlier and have not repented of the impurity (*akatharsia*), sexual immorality (*porneia*), and sensuality (*aselgeia*) that they have practiced.

---

[22] BDAG, 34.

[23] BDAG, 141. "Lack of self-constraint which involves one in conduct that violates all bounds of what is socially acceptable, *self-abandonment*."

Galatians 5:19–21—Now the works of the flesh are evident: sexual immorality (*moicheia*), impurity (*porneia*), sensuality (*akatharsia*), idolatry, sorcery, enmity, strife, jealousy, fits of anger, rivalries, dissensions, divisions, envy, drunkenness, orgies, and things like these. I warn you, as I warned you before, that those who do such things will not inherit the kingdom of God.

Ephesians 4:17–20—Now this I say and testify in the Lord, that you must no longer walk as the Gentiles do, in the futility of their minds. They are darkened in their understanding, alienated from the life of God because of the ignorance that is in them, due to their hardness of heart. They have become callous and have given themselves up to sensuality (*aselgeia*), greedy to practice every kind of impurity (*akatharsia*). But that is not the way you learned Christ!

Ephesians 5:5—For you may be sure of this, that everyone who is sexually immoral (*porneia*) or impure (*akatharsia*), or who is covetous (that is, an idolater), has no inheritance in the kingdom of Christ and God.

Hebrews 13:4—Let marriage be held in honor among all, and let the marriage bed be undefiled, for God will judge the sexually immoral (*porneia*) and adulterous (*moicheia*).

Jude 4—For certain people have crept in unnoticed who long ago were designated for this condemnation, ungodly people, who pervert the grace of our God into sensuality (*aselgeia*) and deny our only Master and Lord, Jesus Christ.

Revelation 21:8—But as for the cowardly, the faithless, the detestable, as for murderers, the sexually immoral (*porneia*), sorcerers, idolaters, and all liars, their portion will be in the lake that burns with fire and sulfur, which is the second death.

The same thoughts come from the pen of Matthew, Paul, Jude, and John (in Revelation). They show the essential danger of improper sexual expressions. Apostolic warnings include both heterosexual sins and homosexual sins. They show the undeniable opposition of such things to the purity of God and the holiness of His Son. Revelation, Hebrews,

Ephesians, and Galatians join together in passing the same sentence of divine condemnation against those who continue in these sins without repentance and turning back to God. This is serious business!

We know from Holy Scripture that God "desires all people to be saved and to come to the knowledge of the truth" (1 Timothy 2:4). While the majority of the passages just reviewed were obviously penned to Christians living in cities scattered throughout the Roman Empire, God's ultimate will is that all people everywhere know His truth. The principles of fidelity, monogamy, and chastity and laws for exclusively heterosexual relations are all rules meant to benefit humanity. Individuals and entire societies suffer when God-given sexual morality is ignored.

When I was invited to lecture on this topic, I was surprised when the professor asked me to address the biblical passages that talk about sex. He wanted his students to hear the biblical witness not as a Word from God to convert them, but as source documents that establish the Christian position. There is a curiosity in the secular world about Christian teaching, and there is a segment of that audience who will be willing to listen to what God's Word says. Examination of the passages addressing sex shows that there is more to God's Word about sex than just prohibitions and laws. Behind those prohibitions is a concern for the souls of individuals, as well as for their peace and well-being in this life. God cares about human suffering, and sexual immorality hurts a lot of people. The passages of the Bible give voice to a higher form of love that empties itself for the sake of the other, a love that points beyond sexual desire and reminds the world of the saving love of God's Son.

One of the greater struggles Christians face when they debate sex and morality with non-Christians is a gross misunderstanding of the biblical witness. Caricatures abound that see Christians as angry zealots wagging their fingers in disapproval at the world and that see the Bible as a book of threats and laws from an age long past. The actual passages in the Bible about sex teach a very different lesson. They present a message about true love tied to God's saving love. They warn about the consequences of breaking God's design not with the spirit of a militant protestor shouting through a bullhorn, but with the spirit of a concerned Father whose wisdom exceeds that of His children. The truth of the Father's wisdom has proven itself throughout the millennia as these apostolic and prophetic words have been repeated to countless generations. Christians need not fear quoting the Bible as they debate the sexual immorality of our age. Both the letter of God's Word and the spirit of grace enfolded with His

Word remain relevant and effective in standing against the dehumanizing effects of sexual hedonism.

Summary

Thus far I have attempted to lay to rest some common misunderstandings about Christian sexual ethics. They are not founded on traditionalism; to the contrary, they have always bucked current social tradition and have been seen as both radical and countercultural. They are also not "safe," inasmuch as those who have espoused them have often found themselves the objects of intense persecution. Christian teachings about sex are more than lists of prohibitions. There is a higher purpose in Christian sexual ethics, namely, to proclaim a Savior whose single-minded love for His fallen people led Him to a life of devotion and self-sacrifice. Christians can find encouragement in the preceding chapters that assures them that their struggles against the tide of sexual hedonism are not in vain. They may not see immediate results from their debate with the world. They may even believe they have lost the day because no one seems to listen, but history has proven that God works though His Word in ways that Christians cannot always see. When Elijah believed he was the last believer left on earth, God assured him that there were still seven thousand who remained faithful (1 Kings 19:18). The masses will undoubtedly not listen to the Christian message, but some will hear, and some will be drawn to Christ over time.

The debate against sexual immorality is much stronger in favor of the biblical position than what most Christians know. Proponents of sexual hedonism claim that science and research are on their side, that unrestrained sexual expression is harmless, and homosexuality is normal. Their propaganda suggests that there are no victims if choices are responsibly and freely made, and they claim further that one's sexual orientation is set at birth and cannot be changed. I've watched Christians be drawn in by these claims and surrender their biblical ethics because they do not have answers to these claims. The goal of the following chapters is to provide some answers to this disinformation and show that things are not as one-sided as the propagandists like to say. The focus in the following chapters will shift more toward the homosexual debate. There are good and credible arguments in favor of Christian teaching from secular sources that help to validate what Christians say about immorality in general and homosexuality in particular.

chapter 4

MOM, DAD, I'M GAY

To begin dealing with the ethics of the secular world, one must understand how different the secular approach is. Christians approach ethical questions by beginning with principles and passages laid down in the Bible. Some of these passages are laws that are both proscriptive and prescriptive in specifying a definite moral code. They tell Christians what to do or what not to do in this or that situation. They define God's standard of ethical purity. Other passages are statements of Gospel that speak of moral chastity and practice in descriptive terms. They describe in ontological language what the Christian now is by virtue of Christ's redemption. Both by the Law and the Gospel the Bible provides an objective basis for judging right and wrong in ethical matters. An objective basis is an identifiable source outside human emotion and feeling; it is a thing that can be accessed equally by all people and is not dependent on human feelings. The Bible is what it is and says what it says, regardless of an individual's subjective and ever-changing emotional state.

A large number of people who challenge biblical teachings do not appear to have an objective basis as their starting point. They do not establish their position based on this or that external authoritative source. Instead, they weigh their conclusions on personal/subjective criteria, like: "Do I like the person involved?" "Does the situation provide an immediate benefit to me or another person?" "Is anyone harmed by the action; if so, who, and does it matter to me?" "Does the action offend me?" This is a sampling of some of the subjective questions that enter the evaluation process as many people address questions of right and wrong. Because the questions are subjective, the answers will vary from person to person.

There is no outside standard by which to measure whose conclusions are best.

As I discuss an issue like homosexuality with people, it is not unusual for them to say something like, "I know a guy who is homosexual, and he is a nice guy who is thoughtful and kind, . . . so how can homosexuality be bad?" Their subjective experience with the individual has decided the question of moral rightness and wrongness for them. If there is enough perceived goodness in a person, then the question of right and wrong becomes largely irrelevant. A person's "likeability" trumps whether his or her moral behavior is right or wrong according to any outside standard. In their estimation, this subjective method of judgment is warm and caring. It considers the feelings and personality of each individual. In contrast, objective methods of judgment, in their view, are cold and uncaring. That is part of the reason why Christian conclusions about morality are rejected outright by society. It is not just the conclusions Christians draw (though it is that too), it is the fact that they weigh their decisions from objective standards that seem cold and indifferent to the needs of individuals.

Thus far in this volume I have discussed ethics from Christian objective standards. I have attempted to demonstrate what God's Word says about sex and morality and how that shapes our understandings. Despite accusations to the contrary, this approach does not disregard individual persons. Just the opposite, it compassionately considers each individual and seeks to give him or her support and direction outside of himself or herself. It directs people to the God of grace who alone can save the lost. Where the subjective whims of society change with the breeze, the objective Word of God endures forever (Isaiah 40:8). The Christian objective approach to determining right and wrong is actually a very sympathetic approach that acknowledges the genuine struggles people face and looks for ways to bring the love of God to them.

As an example, a while back, a man, I'll call him Bob, told me about how he broke the news to his parents that he was gay. He said that his mother replied, "I guess I had always suspected as much." Bob had never married, and it was difficult for him to have close friendships. He struggled with depression and had even contemplated suicide. It was very difficult for him to talk to me about the cross he was bearing. He did it with a great deal of fear because past experiences taught him that religious people often reacted badly to his struggles. People had scolded him and shunned him. Pastors he thought he could trust treated him poorly. I am grateful that he was willing to trust me. Bob helped me understand the struggles of homosexuality from a new and better perspective.

Bob told me that he did not become attracted to men by choice. He struggled to resist his urges. Bob knew all the Bible passages that I cited in the previous chapter, and he agreed with the understanding of them that I presented. He knew homosexuality was sinful and made no effort to defend himself or accuse me of hate crimes because I pointed to Scripture and said God condemns it. One day I told Bob that he was a rare person for admitting homosexuality was wrong when he personally struggled with it. He disagreed with me. He explained that there are many people like him who struggle against their same-sex attractions.

I had assumed that a majority of those who identify as homosexual were content with their sexuality. My experience with the advocates of homosexuality had shown me examples of people who gave no signs of shame or unhappiness with their same-sex attractions. Added to that, my perspective had been fed by the images on TV of people marching in gay-rights parades, shouting to the world that they were gay and proud of it. I had wrongly assumed that they represented a firm majority among the same-sex attracted, but Bob disagreed. He told me there were many people like him who felt their same-sex attractions were like an alien force wrecking their peace of mind and hindering their life with God. He did not want the feelings he had. He tried several different methods of counseling and treatment to rid himself of his feelings. In his experience, there were more people who fought against their homosexual attractions than who embraced them as normal.

Bob's situation begs the question, how do such things happen? How does a person develop an attraction for the same sex that he or she does not want to have? In Bob's case, it was the result of sexual abuse as a child by an older boy in the neighborhood. The boy overpowered Bob and raped him. Bob described feeling dead inside after the rape. Some spark within him was snuffed out to such a degree that he never really recovered. He did not tell anyone for years because of the shame he bore, even though he had not done anything wrong. Many men and women suffering from homosexual impulses have endured traumatic sexual experiences as children. Some of them suppress these experiences and are not even aware of them. Others carry their secret in their memories but will not share them because the pain is so severe.

There is a group of doctors that specializes in psychological therapy for those like Bob who struggle with homosexuality. While I do not completely agree with all their conclusions, I do think that their analysis of possible causes for the development of homosexual tendencies is helpful. Charles Socarides, now deceased, was a professor of psychiatry at the Albert Einstein College of Medicine in the Bronx and a prolific author. He wrote the following;

> I have spent almost my entire professional life on the psycho-dynamics of obligatory homosexuality. Homosexuals aren't born that way. But the seeds of their orientation are sown in their earliest years—before the age of three. They don't re-member what happened to them. So I can understand why some of them might assume, like those of them who are left-handed, that they were born that way. But they weren't. They had smothering mothers and abdicating fathers, and the nor-mal processes of gender identification went awry for them, soul and body. These are the conclusions of a number of systematic, clinical studies comparing homosexuals and heterosexuals, first reported in the psychoanalytic literature of the 1940s, and continuing on into the 1990s.[1]

Socarides documents numerous cases where parents failed to fulfill their role as loving mothers and fathers and confused their children's sexual identity. These cases do not, of course, explain all homosexuality. Bob's confusion, for instance, came later in childhood and was the result of a predatory attack. His parents had nothing to do with it. But these therapists do offer an explanation for some individuals, and they do demonstrate that that sexual identification and attraction can be con-fused through no fault of the person experiencing it. Children, whose ability to understand their circumstances rationally has not yet devel-oped, may internalize their pain in such way that it damages and/or con-fuses their self-image as male or female. It is tragic.

The human psyche can be a very fragile thing. People can be influ-enced and even damaged at the core of their being at any stage in life. Children are especially susceptible, but even adults can find their self-image thrown into chaos by some tragic event. I know of a woman who was engaged to be married and had the wedding day set. Just prior to the wedding, her husband-to-be announced that he was leaving her for an-

---

[1] Charles W. Socarides, *Homosexuality A Freedom Too Far* (Phoenix: Adam Margrave Books, 1995), 100.

other man. Soon after this, the young woman began experimenting with homosexuality. For years she identified as homosexual and was active as a homosexual rights advocate. After more than a decade of being a self-proclaimed homosexual, she married a man, and has, to the best of my knowledge, been living a heterosexual life ever since.

It is important for us as Christians to understand that not all homosexuality is the same. There are many who struggle with same-sex attraction who do not want to feel as they do and who pray constantly for God's help. Some may have been forced into their self-identification because of some early childhood conflict that they themselves might not understand or remember. Others might be the victims of abuse or rape. Others yet might have suffered betrayal by someone they loved.

Of course, I have also run into homosexuals who have not had any parental conflicts, abuse, or sexual betrayals, and who are very comfortable with their homosexuality. They resent the suggestion that their sexuality is the result of something that has gone wrong in their lives. They believe their homosexuality is normal, and they are quite comfortable with it. Unfortunately, it is this group that is most often presented as the status quo of homosexuality. They are the group most likely to seize the spotlight and claim to represent all homosexuals. Christians do a great disservice to those who seek Christ's grace and mercy by lumping all same-sex attracted people into one group. There are many who live in daily repentance and seek God's grace. They live celibate lives, and though they struggle with attractions to those of their own gender, they do not act upon these temptations.

The objective standards of God's Word that clearly condemn homosexual sins do not prevent Christians from helping those who struggle with sexual sins. God's Word teaches that through Christ's atonement, there is forgiveness for all sexual sins, and in forgiveness God can and does change lives. Those who understand that their homosexual tendencies are at odds with the will of God and who seek God's forgiveness need to hear that Jesus understands the profound brokenness of their human flesh. He died as an offering for their sins the same as for all the many heterosexual sins of the world. God loves them. God forgives them, and God's Holy Spirit will continue to work within them to overcome sin. Repentance works the same for anyone and for any sexual sin. It is a genuine turning away from the offense and turning toward God for new life. Repentance requires constant resistance to that sinful desire and a heartfelt searching for ways to lessen such feelings. Repentance translates into struggle that may last one's entire life, but it is a struggle under the grace and constant forgiveness of a Savior who knows the weakness of our flesh and chooses to love us anyway.

The struggles of repentant men and women who deal with same-sex attraction can, in some ways, be more heartfelt than what many heterosexual people feel. How many men take an extra glance at a beautiful woman who walks by, or make comments to a buddy about the anatomy of this or that woman, or lust after a woman on TV or at the beach, or look at dirty pictures online? The fact is, heterosexuals are constantly allowing their desires for the opposite sex to pull them into sin, but most do not feel all that shameful for it. They may act as if it is normal and therefore acceptable. Whereas a person who is same-sex attracted might pour his or her heart out to God every night asking for help against improper thoughts, a heterosexual might not see his lustful thoughts, glances, and jokes as sins in need of forgiveness. The many verses we explored in chapter 3 should make clear that in God's eyes, any and all sexual sins are violations of God's will. Heterosexual lust is just as sinful as homosexual lust, and it can be just as damaging to the self and people around that individual.

The role of the church

The Church was designed by God to be a hospital for sick souls. There is no doubt that among the many Gentile converts living in the Greco-Roman cities where Paul ministered, some had been involved in homosexual acts. The congregations begun by Paul were meant to be places of refuge where sinful people of every stripe could come to be reconciled to God.

Paul's normal method for beginning a congregation was to find the Jewish synagogue in the city and start teaching there. Often he was expelled from the synagogue and regrouped at a different location with a small core of followers (cf. Acts 13:14–46; 14:1–7; 17:1–9; 18:1–11). The congregations that began from this were made up of people who were disenfranchised by the status quo and often lived under a cloud of social hostility. They faced pressures from the Jewish community for believing in things the majority rejected, and they were rejected by the dominant Roman culture for not being accepting of Rome's gods. They were in conflict from the outside and conflicted on the inside as each person brought his or her unique sinful baggage into the Church. These pressures forced them closer together as they supported and strengthened each other against their shared enemies. In his epistles to the Romans and Corinthians, Paul uses the image of a human body to teach his new Christian converts about their need to help and support one another in their weaknesses.

> The eye cannot say to the hand, "I have no need of you," nor again the head to the feet, "I have no need of you." On the contrary, the parts of the body that seem to be weaker are indispensable, and on those parts of the body that we think less honorable we bestow the greater honor, and our unpresentable parts are treated with greater modesty, which our more presentable parts do not require. But God has so composed the body, giving greater honor to the part that lacked it, that there may be no division in the body, but that the members may have the same care for one another. If one member suffers, all suffer together; if one member is honored, all rejoice together. Now you are the body of Christ and individually members of it. (1 Corinthians 12:21–27; cf. Romans 12:3–17)

The Church is Christ's answer to every individual's struggle. It is the place where those who are guilty can find support from fellow guilty "strugglers." Within the Church, no one is better than anyone else; no one is less guilty of sin. All are in need of the forgiving love of Christ to reconcile them with God the Father. The Church is the perfect place for conflicted individuals to find peace with God and with other people who likewise need forgiveness.

Those who are struggling against same-sex attractions may be hesitant to come to Church because they are afraid of being condemned or shunned by other members. They may have had bad experiences like my friend Bob, but they need the love of God and the fellowship of other Christians the same as every heterosexual man and woman. Through forgiveness given in Baptism, at His Supper, and through His word of absolution, God reconciles all people to Himself in equal measure. He gives His Holy Spirit in the same way to all people who are repentant to help them in their struggles. It is vital that people who struggle with sexual sins be confident that they will find true brothers and sisters in the Church who care about them and support them.

matthew 19 and eunuchs

It may be easier for members of the Church to act compassionately toward those who suffer with sexual sins if they recognize the pervasive sexual pressure our culture places on everyone. The Church today needs to take special care with this because the world has changed and these matters are greater problems for our generation than for previous generations. Sean McDowell and John Stonestreet have noted the enormity of the problem for our generation in their book *Same-Sex Marriage*. They call it a "cosmological shift" that has taken place in western culture.[2] People are taught to define themselves first and foremost as sexual beings.

> The historic Western understanding of the human person was that we are fundamentally religious creatures. This doesn't mean that everyone in the history of Western civilization agreed on religion or believed in the same religious ideals, but that it was commonly held that the most important thing about humans is the metaphysical search for the meaning and purpose of life. For many, this was considered more fundamental to human identity than physical survival or sexual pleasures. In other words, humans were humans because they wrestled with the big, ultimate questions of existence. . . . Now, every view of sexuality is rooted in metaphysical assumptions about the meaning of life and human identity. But the quest to wrestle with and answer the ultimate questions has been preempted by the conclusion now demanded of everyone up front: sexuality is who we are.[3]

This is a grassroots worldview problem that meets kids on the playground and in the classroom. Boys and girls are taught to judge each other in sexual terms. They are expected to exhibit appropriate amounts of sexual behavior almost from the womb. If a young boy does not show the expected amount of interest in girls or exhibit enough aggression, or if he would rather play with stuffed animals than toy trucks, he might be told by other kids that he is "gay." A friend of mine who is now married

---

[2] Sean McDowell and John Stonestreet, *Same-Sex Marriage* (Grand Rapids, MI: Baker Books, 2014), 68.

[3] McDowell and Stonestreet, *Same-Sex Marriage*, 68–69.

with children told me how as a child he was called "gay" by other kids. He was not interested in sports as a kid and therefore was not very athletic. He was a good student and somewhat bookish, and during his younger years, he did not show a great deal of interest in girls. He also did not join in with other boys when they made vulgar jokes about girls. Other students made fun of him and called him "gay." It was not until after high school, when he went to college, that his interest in the opposite sex was piqued by a young lady whom he eventually married.

This cultural pressure even on the playground to identify oneself in sexual terms is the fruit of the "cosmological shift" in thinking. Boys and girls see themselves first and foremost as sexual beings who must present themselves in sexual ways to appease the sexual expectations of the society around them. The more aggressively they pursue the opposite sex, the more they assure themselves that they are "normal." I've had people ask me if I thought some young man was homosexual because he never dated and apparently was not that interested in women. But the lack of someone's level of interest in the opposite sex is no measure of latent homosexuality any more than that person's aggressive pursuit of the opposite sex is a guarantee of his or her heterosexuality. A young man I knew in high school was very attracted to the young women in school and pursued them with a passion. He boasted about having sex with a number of young women, most of whom were quite willing to confirm his stories. He was also very open and rude about hating homosexuals. Now, thirty years later, he is a self-professed homosexual.

The cultural pressure to see oneself first and foremost as a sexual being becomes all the more difficult to resist when it is taught by adults to children. Sex education in schools builds on this fundamental cultural belief that everyone is born a "sexual being."[4] It claims to help and guide children in understanding their sexuality by discussing sex and encouraging acceptance of different expressions of sexuality. Children may be subjected to graphic discussions and pictures of sexual acts. They may be shown videos of "safe sex" in action. They may be asked to draw

---

[4] The concept of being sexual from birth and seeking one's identity primarily through sexuality has been championed by the formers of sex education. For an in-depth discussion of this, see Linda Bartlett, *The Failure of Sex Education in the Church* (Iowa Falls, IA: Titus 2 for Life, 2014), 12–13.

pictures of their own sexual organs to share with the teacher.[5] At every stage, children are encouraged to surrender their shyness and shed their modesty about sexual matters. Rome had its gymnasium to rob children of their innocence and inhibitions; this generation has sex-education classes in schools. As part and parcel of these classes, children are encouraged to be accepting of homosexual identity. They are taught that homosexuality is as normal as heterosexuality. Any discussion of right or wrong in the eyes of God is strictly forbidden. The secular humanism behind much of the sex-education curricula claims it would be wrong to bring religious standards into the classroom. Ironically, they fail to recognize that secular humanism is itself a religious conviction.

These sexual pressures upon children from the classroom to the soccer field and from friends to teachers drive children to think of themselves as sexual beings first and foremost. They are pressured to evaluate their own sexual feelings and sexual identities. Children who otherwise may not have given a second thought to sex are pushed into having sexual thoughts they are simply not mature enough to evaluate. Not surprisingly, many children find themselves badgered into utter confusion about their own sexual identity. Some children become convinced that they must identify as homosexual because they do not fit the mold of typical heterosexual behavior that someone has determined they should fit.

A passage often overlooked in the discussion of sexual identity in children is Matthew 10:12. In this passage, Jesus was being questioned about marriage and divorce, but His answer applies far beyond the strict discussion of marriage; it actually touches on the sexual identity of children. Jesus concluded His discussion with the following statement:

> For there are eunuchs who have been so from birth, and there are eunuchs who have been made eunuchs by men, and there are eunuchs who have made themselves eunuchs for the sake of the kingdom of heaven. Let the one who is able to receive this receive it.

A eunuch was a male who had been physically castrated. Castration was not an uncommon practice in Jesus' day. There were a number of

---

[5] An assignment I was actually given in high school "health" class, which I refused to do. Several students fulfilled this assignment by photocopying their private parts and turning in the copies.

reasons why men were castrated. In Roman culture, castration was a way of prolonging adolescence. If a Roman man was in a pederast relationship with his slave boy, for instance, he might castrate the slave in order to slow the maturation process and the onset of puberty. The end of pederast relationships was usually marked by hair growth at puberty; castration delayed that. Besides castration serving sexual goals in Roman culture, there was also the practice of castration for servants assigned to special roles within affluent households. Men who were assigned to watch over women might be castrated as a way of ensuring they could be trusted alone with women in the house.

As Jesus uses the term *eunuch*, He has both literal and figurative meanings in mind. He speaks of three categories of eunuchs: those born that way, those made such by the hands of men, and those who have made themselves eunuchs for the sake of the kingdom of God. It seems clear enough that the second group, those who were made eunuchs by the hands of men, should be taken literally. They were castrated physically because someone willed it. The third group, those who are eunuchs for the sake of the kingdom of God, seems less likely to be literal. Jesus most certainly is referring to men, like St. Paul, who chose a life of celibacy in order to serve God more fully and not be hindered by responsibilities to a wife or family.[6]

Paul speaks to his own celibacy in 1 Corinthians 7:7–9, "I wish that all were as I myself am. But each has his own gift from God, one of one kind and one of another. To the unmarried and the widows I say that it is good for them to remain single as I am. But if they cannot exercise self-control, they should marry. For it is better to marry than to burn with passion." Paul sees celibacy as a special gift, not a command. It is a gift inasmuch as it allowed him to devote all his energies into serving God and the Church. Yet Paul recognized that it is not for everyone. "But if they cannot exercise self-control, they should marry."

I have only known a handful of men in my life who were comfortable with a life of celibacy. A Greek professor in my college days was one such man. One day, we students, curious about his being single, asked him why he never married. He said that there was a time in his life when he was very serious with a young lady and was contemplating marriage.

---

[6] Cf. Jeffrey Gibbs, *Concordia Commentary: Matthew* (St. Louis: Concordia, 2010), 954–955. Gibbs's discussion supports the figurative reading of eunuch with reference to the third group. He does not, however, consider how a figurative reading at this place may impact the causal understanding of the first group.

However, he realized that if he married, he would not be able to devote all his time and efforts to the study of Greek. To do justice to either his studies or wife, he had to choose one over the other; he chose Greek. He said he never regretted his decision and was very fulfilled in his life as a Classics professor. God granted him the special gift of not needing female companionship. Celibacy is not an easy life. But as Jesus noted in Matthew 19, it is an avenue that some do choose as a means of being able to serve God more fully. Luther, too, understood that those who were made eunuchs by men were literally castrated; while those who chose to be eunuchs for the kingdom's sake were celibate.

> The first and second classes are those who either were born that way or were castrated by the hands of men. They are called "castrates" by the world and the jurists, too. But the third class are those who have castrated themselves for the sake of the kingdom of heaven. They are another kind of castrate; they are called eunuchs not outwardly, in their body, but spiritually, in their heart, not in a worldly sense, but as He says, "for the sake of the kingdom of heaven."[7]

Especially interesting for this discussion of sexual identity is Jesus' first category, those who were born that way. It is certainly possible, as Luther understood it, that Jesus is talking about a physical issue. To suffer from such a condition from birth means there would be some physical defect where boys were literally deprived of the normal function of male sexual organs. Such a defect, through no fault of their own, would cause serious developmental problems and would affect their desires for the opposite sex. But it is also possible that this first category could include those who, from birth, simply do not have an active desire to be with the opposite sex. Jesus has demonstrated that the term *eunuch* can be applied in a figurative sense to those who choose celibacy to serve God. Why can it not also include those who are born with a penchant for celibacy because they do not feel the need to chase the opposite gender?

There are people who just are not that interested in dating or marriage. There is no reason why this text could not include them. They are eunuchs in a figurative way, born without a strong impulse for marriage or family. *That does not mean they are homosexual!* Jesus does not condemn those who are not interested sexually in the opposite sex,

---

[7] Martin Luther, *Luther's Works*, vol. 21 (St. Louis: Concordia, 1956), 90.

and He does not classify such "eunuchs" as "homosexual." A eunuch represents someone who is either in control over his sexual urges through the force of his sanctified will or someone who simply lacks a strong sex drive. It is not a term for someone whose sexual desire is for those of his own gender. There is no biblical text that would support the view that people are born homosexual. That being said, those who do not feel a particular attraction for the other sex can be directed to this passage for assurance that there is nothing sinful in lacking an "alpha male" sex drive. Jesus recognizes the state of being a eunuch and does not condemn them for being born without a strong desire for the opposite sex.

In a world driving children to stake out their sexual identity, it can be of great comfort to assure children that they do not have to adopt a sexual worldview. It is okay if they have feelings for the opposite sex and okay if those feelings do not seem as pronounced as other children. They are not defined by the feelings they have in the moment. They are redeemed children of the Savior who will shape and mold them over time into a God-pleasing image. If they have thoughts or feelings that are contrary to God's will, God can forgive that and redirect them to more God-pleasing thoughts.

Temptation and Sin

It is also important when we speak about individuals suffering with same-sex attraction that we make a distinction between being tempted by sin and yielding to it. Temptation is not the same as sin. Temptations play on those elements of our inner being that have a weakness for a certain sin, but in and of themselves temptations are not sins.

It goes without saying, but maybe needs to be said, that the sexual sins Paul lists and condemns in his epistles would not suddenly cease to be temptations for people. As human beings, Paul's new converts would continue to have improper urges and desires. I doubt they could walk down the streets of the city without having all the sins they used to love and practice waved under their noses. In art, in conversation with friends, by seeing prostitutes on the streets, sexual temptations would have surrounded them. But as baptized Christians, those temptations did not define them.

Temptations of all kinds are a regular part of fallen human nature. We cannot avoid them; nor does facing temptation make us guilty of committing sin. Being able to resist temptation confirms Christ's work.

Luther takes pains in his Large Catechism to differentiate between temptation and sin. Luther wrote:

> To feel temptation is, therefore, a far different thing from consenting or yielding to it. We must all feel it, although not all in the same way. Some feel it in a greater degree and more severely than others. For example, the young suffer especially from the flesh. Afterward, when they reach middle life and old age, they feel it from the world. But others who are occupied with spiritual matters, that is, strong Christians, feel it from the devil. Such feeling, as long as it is against our will and we would rather be rid of it, can harm no one. For if we did not feel it, it could not be called a temptation. But we consent to it when we give it the reins and do not resist it or pray against it.
>
> Therefore, we Christians must be armed [Ephesians 6:10–18] and daily expect to be constantly attacked. No one may go on in security and carelessly, as though the devil were far from us. At all times we must expect and block his blows. Though I am now chaste, patient, kind, and in firm faith, the devil will this very hour send such an arrow into my heart that I can scarcely stand. For he is an enemy that never stops or becomes tired. So when one temptation stops, there always arise others and fresh ones.
>
> So there is no help or comfort except to run here, take hold of the Lord's Prayer, and speak to God from the heart like this: "Dear Father, You have asked me to pray. Don't let me fall because of temptations." Then you will see the temptations must stop and finally confess themselves conquered. If you try to help yourself by your own thoughts and counsel, you will only make the matter worse and give the devil more space. For he has a serpent's head [Revelation 12:9]. If it finds an opening into which it can slip, the whole body will follow without stopping. But prayer can prevent him and drive him back.[8]

I've heard many Christians say that homosexuality is not in itself a sin, it only becomes a sin as one acts upon it. But that is not exactly what

---

[8] *Concordia: The Lutheran Confessions*, ed. Paul McCain (St. Louis: Concordia, 2006), 421.

Luther says, nor is it biblically accurate. Temptation is not sin, but desire for what is forbidden is. God's Word does not condemn only actions as sin. In speaking of heterosexual sin, Jesus said, "Everyone who looks at a woman with lustful intent has already committed adultery with her in his heart" (Matthew 5:28). Improper sexual desire is in itself contrary to the will of God and is therefore sinful. That applies to both heterosexual and homosexual desires. Lust of any kind is sin. What is not sin is being tempted to lust.

Temptation is an invitation to let go of what is right in God's eyes and embrace what is against God. For a heterosexual man, seeing a beautiful women in a scanty dress is a temptation to lust. He can look at her without sin if he is able in his heart to repress his sexual thoughts and see her simply as a beautiful human being. However, if he "undresses her with his eyes," and lets his thoughts imagine her as a sexual partner, or thinks of her in a sexual way, the temptation has become a sin. Most people with strong heterosexual desires cross that line and sin against the opposite gender many times a day. They need constant forgiveness from Christ and the persistent help of the Holy Spirit to overcome their lusts.

It is no different for those whose sinful weakness is toward homosexual sins. Inner urges can be and should be repressed when they are not in accord with God's Word. Any sexual desire for someone of the same sex is a forbidden desire and therefore sin. People with a weakness to homosexuality can interact and live among people of the same sex without sinning. They can see others of their gender as human beings on their own merits. However, when they give in to forbidden thoughts and "undress the other with their eyes" or imagine him or her as a sexual partner, or think of that person in a sexual way, then they have crossed the line into sin the same as any heterosexual would (cf. James 1:13–15). There is only one God-pleasing context for sexual desire, and that is within heterosexual marriage. This is why Paul tells the Corinthians who struggle with sexual temptations, "But if they cannot exercise self-control, they should marry. For it is better to marry than to burn with passion" (1 Corinthians 7:9).

We human beings are weak creatures. Temptations turn into sins more often than they should. We fall when we should be strong and resist the voice of sin that tells us to ignore what God says. It is the nature of our sinful humanity. However, the fact that we are weak does not mean that our situation is hopeless. Paul preached forgiveness as the antidote to our sinfulness. He pointed to Christ as the One who knew the terrible state of the human heart. Jesus knows what we are inside. He sees how often we fall, which is why He made Himself the offering we need and why He has given us His Church with its proclamation of His Gospel and application of His Sacraments. Members of the Church have the support of fellow Christians who are struggling with their own sins. Broken people living under grace help other broken people to remember that they, too, live under grace. The shared liturgy, the proclamation of God's Word, the reception of the Lord's Supper shoulder to shoulder with other Christians is meant to be a source of strength and help against temptations.

Forgiveness from Christ does more than just erase the record of past sins. Forgiveness is the way God places His Holy Spirit within His people to take up that inner fight they wage. God's Spirit allows the man who lusts after women to look at a woman and not give in to his weakness, to turn his eyes away, and not let his imagination run wild. God's Spirit works within the man or woman whose weakness is for those of the same sex. He helps them to resist improper thoughts and actions. God Himself becomes our strength that stands against the sinful weakness that lurks within our hearts. Christians are not less sinful than non-Christians, but they do have a Savior who both forgives sins and fights within them against the temptations in their path.

Having a weakness toward homosexual sins does not mean that person should think of him or herself as homosexual. With forgiveness comes new being, new self-identity, new direction and strength. The Christian life is a life of self-denial. Every Christian daily denies those elements of the sinful flesh that want to stray from God. I suggested to my friend who was repentant about his same-sex attractions that he should not call himself a homosexual, because in Christ his same-sex attractions were forgiven and should not therefore define him. He agreed that Jesus' redemption did cover all his sins, but he struggled to give up the tag of homosexual. He said that everybody talks that way. It would be too confusing for others who struggled with same-sex attraction if he said he was not homosexual anymore. I respect his struggle, but I disagree with this concern over causing confusion. I do not think it is bad to shake things up that need shaking up. It would be good for people to understand that in Christ they can see themselves differently than the world sees them. Forgiven Christians are not the sum of their sins. They are washed, made holy, justified, and forgiven through Christ. Just because one is tempted by a certain sin should not make him or her feel like he or she must identify with that sin.

homosexuality and orientation

There are other places where I believe terms and concepts should be shaken up. The prevailing language about sexual "orientation" sends a wrong message that needs correcting. "Orientation" is usually meant to express the belief that sexuality is an essential element of one's personal identity that cannot be changed because it is bound up in the very biology of the individual. It is a matter of being or ontology, and as such, is beyond the control of an individual.

This mindset is actually legally codified in Iowa, where I live. In 2009, in its ruling to legalize same-sex marriage, the Iowa Supreme Court stated that sexuality is to be considered as an immutable trait and therefore a matter to be protected under law.

> A human trait that defines a group is "immutable" when the trait exists "solely by the accident of birth," *Frontiero v. Richardson*, 411 U.S. 677, 686, 93 S. Ct. 1764, 1770, 36 L. Ed. 2d 583, 591 (1973) (Brennan, J., plurality opinion), or when the person with the trait has no ability to change it, *Regents of Univ. of Cal. v. Bakke*, 438 U.S. 265, 360, 98 S. Ct. 2733, 2784, 57 L. Ed. 2d 750, 815 (1978).[9]

> Accordingly, because sexual orientation is central to personal identity and "may be altered [if at all] only at the expense of significant damage to the individual's sense of self," classifications based on sexual orientation "are no less entitled to consideration as a suspect or quasi-suspect class than any other group that has been deemed to exhibit an immutable characteristic."[10]

In the first paragraph cited above, the court gives the historic definition of immutability as a trait that "exists solely by the accident of birth" (like one's race, gender, or birth abnormality) or as a trait that cannot be changed (like a disability). In order to accommodate sexuality

---

[9] Varnum v. Brien, No. 07–1499, IA, 42 (April 2009).
[10] Varnum v. Brien, No. 07–1499, IA, 44 (April 2009).

under the legal umbrella of immutability, the court, in the second paragraph, redefines the historic definition of immutability. Under the new definition, a trait is immutable when changing it may result in "significant damage to the individual's sense of self." The historic definition of immutability is objective and can be verified. It is based on standards that can be established through hard science. The new definition of immutability, however, is wholly subjective and cannot be verified by any scientific means. It opens the door for virtually any interpretation. For instance, who is to say that someone who is sexually attracted to adolescent boys or girls or multiple partners does not consider this to be part of his or her individual sense of self, which if altered, would significantly harm his or her self-image? One can plug any sexually aberrant behavior desired into the new definition of immutability; and it should, therefore, be protected by law.

The ramifications of this definition of immutability became apparent in June of 2015 in the ruling of the Supreme Court of the United States that legalized same-sex marriage throughout the country. Twice in their ruling they use the term *immutable* in reference to homosexual attraction.[11] Defining immutability in the way that courts are now doing lends strength to the myth that sexuality is immutable, that is, that it cannot be changed without significant damage to one's sense of self. Someone who is tempted by homosexual sins may now find justification for the belief that he or she is and always will be that way because sexuality is immutable.

We need to challenge, even reject, the notion of immutability as an element of sexual "orientation." The fact of the matter is that people can and do change their sexual "orientation." There are scores of people, some with whom I as a pastor have had firsthand dealings, who once considered themselves heterosexual, who were married and had children, but then decided they were homosexual. Their sexuality was not immutable in their move from heterosexual to homosexual, and no one seems to be arguing that they cannot become homosexual because it may damage their sense of self. I also know of several women who claimed to be homosexual and who lived in homosexual relationships but then decided that they were not homosexual anymore and took up relationships with men. Real life provides plenty of evidence that

---

[11] Obergefell v. Hodges No. 14–556 (U.S. June 26, 2015), 4 and 8.

sexuality is not immutable. Consider the following observation from a psychiatry text:

> Some persons change from heterosexual to homosexual or the reverse in their thirties, forties, or fifties. Some remain bisexual during their adult lives. Observations of human sexual behavior . . . have suggested that sexual orientation and identity are not static. In fact, both may fluctuate over a person's lifetime. Sometimes changes in sexuality are "just phases"; sometimes they become the predominant disposition of sexual relation.[12]

Dr. Jeffrey Satinover, who has degrees from MIT, Harvard, and the University of Texas and who served as a Fellow in Psychiatry and Child Psychiatry at Yale University, notes that studies on human sexuality show that "homosexuality tended spontaneously to 'convert' into heterosexuality as a cohort of individuals aged, and this was true for both men and women—the pull of the normative, as it were."[13] He goes on to say:

> The reality is that since 1994—for 10 years—there has existed solid epidemiologic evidence, now extensively confirmed and reconfirmed, that the most common natural course for a young person who develops a "homosexual identity" is for it to spontaneously disappear unless that process is discouraged or interfered with by extraneous factors. We may now say with increasing confidence that those "extraneous" factors are primarily the "social milieu" in which the person finds himself.[14]

---

[12] Tasman, Kay, and Lieberman, *Psychiatry*, vol. 2, 2nd ed. (Australia: John Wiley and Sons Ltd., 2003), 1802. Copyright © 2003 John Wiley and Sons Ltd.

[13] Jeffrey Satinover, "How the Mental Health Associations Misrepresent Science" in Daniel R. Heimbach, *Why Not Same-Sex Marriage* (Sisters, OR: Trusted Books, 2014), 426. Satinover cites the results of the following comprehensive study: Laumann, Gagnon, Michael, and Michaels, *The Social Organization of Sexuality: Sexual Practices in the United States* (Chicago: University of Chicago Press, 1994). On page 283 of this study, presuppositions are labeled as patently false which claim that homosexuality is a "uniform attribute" for all individuals and that homosexual attraction is always stable over time. The authors of this study observe that people's attractions do change. Therefore measuring a percent of the population that is strictly homosexual is difficult if not impossible.

[14] Satinover, "How the Mental Health Associations Misrepresent Science" in *Why Not Same-Sex Marriage*, 447.

On the website of the NARTH Institute (National Association for Research and Therapy of Homosexuality), there are numerous articles and first-hand accounts of homosexuals changing their "orientation" and living in healthy heterosexual relationships. Citing a study by Whitehead and Whitehead (2011), they claim that men who are exclusively heterosexual are seventeen times more stable in their attraction than men who identify as exclusively homosexual. Women whose attractions are exclusively heterosexual are thirty times more likely to remain stable than women who claim to be exclusively homosexual.[15] In other words, it is much more common for those who are exclusively same-sex attracted (homosexual) to change and become opposite-sex attracted (heterosexual) than for those who are exclusively opposite-sex attracted to become same-sex attracted.

Despite the strong evidence, it is common for those supporting homosexuality to make the claim that all attempts to move from homosexual to heterosexual either result in failure or in severe damage to the emotional/psychological being of the individuals involved. Such claims are mere rhetoric and propaganda. They are not rooted in fact. However, the propaganda is extremely effective because it is repeated so often and with such conviction. Sexual immutability is simply a given among the majority. One is "born that way" and therefore cannot change.

The way the term *sexual orientation* is used in popular conversation is packed with baggage that essentially denies the power of grace. Grace can and does redefine people and can and does give them strength over the temptations they face. If homosexuality is immutable, then God is the author of sin, because individuals are helpless against their own biology. Instead of using the language of "orientation" or "immutability" we would be better served using the term *sexual identity,* or in the case of those whose homosexual leanings are a result of conscious choices, *gender preference.* "Preference" points to an act of the will. Those who had considered themselves heterosexual and only after exposure to homosexual experimentation or influence decided they were homosexual have exercised their will. They decided to be homosexual. The term *sexual identity* is slightly different, in that it recognizes some people have been driven to a sexual attraction quite apart from their active will.

---

[15] National Association for Research and Therapy of Homosexuality, *Frequently Asked Questions,* "Can change occur in a person's sexual attractions or orientation?" www.narth.com/#!faq/cirw (accessed January 26, 2016).

Sin, while being part of our human nature after the fall, is not immutable according to the court's definition. That is, it is something that can be changed and altered without damaging our inner self. In fact, as Christians, we depend on Christ to overcome what we are born as and create a new thing within us that frees our true selves. Changing from the way we were into redeemed children of Christ does not damage us, it releases us to enjoy the fullness of God's love. The language of "orientation" and "immutability" denies the essential Christian truth of the Gospel. It creates a false understanding that sexual sins are so tied to one's being that there can be no change. Proclaiming the Gospel to those caught in sexual sins demands that we challenge these common secular views even if they are codified by human law. Change is exactly what all Christians depend upon from God. He must change us at the core of our being and redirect our lives to Him, or there is no hope of salvation.

Summary

It is important that Christians be more than "Bible thumpers," as we are sometimes accused of being. Quoting a bunch of verses that condemn homosexuality to people who struggle with same-sex attraction may serve only to drive them further from God. We must be aware that context determines meaning even in individual people. Not all who identify as homosexual are the same. Some genuinely struggle against same-sex attraction and affirm God's Word that speaks against homosexuality. Others are militant in their homosexuality and close their ears to any mention of the Bible. A sensitive approach to those in need is a must. Those who do not believe their same-sex desires are sinful need to hear from God's Word that homosexual desire and action is contrary to God's will. Those who want help against same-sex attraction need to hear the Gospel of Christ that gives them Jesus' grace to cover their sins and help them through their struggles. Being willing to listen first and discern the actual situation of individuals goes a long way in applying God's Word correctly.

chapter 5

A MIXED BAG OF OBJECTIONS

When I first began my doctoral studies, my advisor offered me the advice, "Beware the sound of one hand clapping." What he meant was that both sides of an argument need to be considered. It is bad scholarship to try to make one's point without giving serious consideration to the other side of the debate. I have listened to the proponents of homosexuality as they have made their case for acceptance, heard their objections to my position, and invited discussion and disagreement. I have read articles and books that are contrary to Christian sexual ethics, all in an attempt to listen to both hands clapping.

One of the things that has become painfully clear in my conversations with the proponents of homosexual acceptance is that this basic rule is not that important to many of them. I have been told by several individuals that they do not really care what the Bible has to say and do not consider it relevant to their position. They put up a wall to the Christian position and see no reason to consider it seriously. Sadly, what many know of the Word of God is what they see on TV about the Bible or what they have read against Christianity. More often than not, it is a terrible caricature of biblical teaching. Just this week, as I was reclining in the dentist chair, my dentist was describing the show he watched on the Bible the night before. He clearly enjoyed it and asked his assistant if she saw it. She said she had not and asked him if it was accurate to the Bible. His answer was "I don't know." His hands were in my mouth so I could not comment, but I wanted to say, "That's the problem with watching shows about the Bible without ever reading the Bible." People do not know what the Bible actually teaches, so they do not know if what they see or hear is a fair picture of it. They assume it must be if someone took the time to present it, but often it is not.

This is the culture in which Christians try to debate issues like homosexuality. It is a culture that does not care about addressing biblical concerns seriously. Many approach the issue with a preconditioned hostility toward religion in general. At the beginning of one lecture, I asked those present to raise their hands if they had a negative impression of me because I was wearing a clerical collar. Over half the room raised their hands. I thanked them for being honest, and then used the situation to suggest that preconceived notions make honest communication more difficult. Approaching the other side with hostility creates an atmosphere where all one will hear is the sound of one hand clapping. If Christians are going to debate this issue effectively, they have to listen to the other side. There is evidence brought against the Christian position that comes from scientific and sociological research that Christians need to know and know how to answer. There are also accusations against the Christian position that sound factual but fail to consider important information to the contrary. Christians need to have some idea how to answer unfair attacks. Simply shutting off the arguments of the pro-homosexual crowd will not convince anyone whose mind may be open to discussion.

In this chapter, I will share several of the more common arguments I have heard. These objections to biblical teachings have come up repeatedly in my discussions. The examples I offer are not meant to be exhaustive, only to present a sampling of what I have encountered. These are issues that one would be likely to face anywhere. Hopefully, a brief review of them will provide some possible answers for others who might find themselves facing similar objections.

inconsistency in applying the law

The first accusation is not the result of misrepresenting God's Word; it is more a simple matter of ignorance. On several occasions, I have been told that Christians are hypocritical when applying the laws of the Bible. Christians seem to pick and choose which laws they want to follow and which they will simply ignore. For example, a young man in the audience once asked me if I liked shellfish. I said I did, whereupon he accused me of hypocrisy, because Leviticus 11:9–10 says,

These you may eat, of all that are in the waters. Everything in the waters that has fins and scales, whether in the seas or in the rivers, you may eat. But anything in the seas or the rivers that does not have fins and scales, of the swarming creatures in the waters and of the living creatures that are in the waters, is detestable to you. You shall regard them as detestable; you shall not eat any of their flesh, and you shall detest their carcasses.

He could not understand how I could claim that laws about sexuality were binding but laws on foods were not. It is a valid question. He was not purposely misrepresenting Christianity; he just did not understand the distinction in laws, and he is not alone. Many church-going people do not know why the church follows some laws but not others. The answer is that not all biblical laws are the same. Biblical laws can be divided into ceremonial, civil, and moral laws.[1] All three types of law were divinely commanded. They were all to be followed with the same rigor in the Old Testament. But with the coming of Christ, the laws of the Old Testament took on a new dimension. Some laws no longer applied, because their purpose was fulfilled. Other laws were still in effect, but the relationship of Christians to them had changed.

CEREMONIAL LAW

The ceremonial law dealt with the worship life and ceremonies of ancient Israel. It had to do with sacrifices, feasts, foods, the priesthood, conduct for worship, purity laws, and circumcision. Ceremonial laws tended to be highly symbolic, pointing beyond the doing of the law to greater truths about the gracious workings of God.[2] Certain ceremonial laws pointed directly to the Messiah and His saving work. They also were a reminder of the price of sin.[3]

For example, Exodus 12 provided the Jews with God's instructions about the Passover meal. It was a meal He told the Israelites to perform annually to remember their deliverance from Egypt. At the heart of this meal was a male lamb. The law said the lamb was supposed to be a year

---

[1] For a discussion on these categories by both Melanchthon and Chemnitz, see Martin Chemnitz, *Loci Theologici*, vol. 2, trans. J. A. O. Preus (St. Louis: Concordia, 1973), 342, 343.

[2] Johann Gerhard, *On the Law of God*, trans. Richard Dinda (St. Louis: Concordia, 2015), 277–278.

[3] Cf. Chemnitz, *Loci Theologici*, 345.

old and without blemish (Exodus 12:5). The law also told people to kill it at twilight, roast it over fire, and eat it in haste. That lamb is shown to have symbolic importance in the New Testament when it is connected to Christ. The New Testament calls Jesus the "Lamb of God" (John 1:29; Revelation 5:6, 8, 12, 13). The shedding of Jesus' blood coincided with the shedding the blood of the Passover lamb (Mark 14:12ff.). The Old Testament laws about the Passover, then, were intended to foreshadow Christ. Once He fulfilled the symbols by actually shedding His blood as the sacrifice for sins, the old symbolism was no longer needed. The Christian Church following the death of Christ did not continue the ceremonial practices of Passover.

Sabbath laws are another example of ceremonial laws losing their force with the coming of Christ. Laws governing the Sabbath directed not only the day on which people were to worship (Saturday) but what they could or could not do on that day. There could be no baking or cooking on the Sabbath (Exodus 16:23). All people, servants, and even animals were not supposed to do any kind of work (Exodus 20:23). The Jews were not to start fires in their dwellings (Exodus 35:3). Breaking these laws incurred the death penalty. Beyond the weekly Sabbath, there was also a Sabbath year, when every seventh year the land was to lay fallow (Exodus 23:11). Farmers were to store up enough grain in previous years to carry the population through a Sabbath year when no farms produced.

Sabbath laws were more than God's way of giving His creatures a break one day a week to be refreshed. The Sabbath was intended to remind people of God's creative work (Exodus 20:8–11). He created for six days and rested on the seventh because all He did was good. The Sabbath also symbolized the spiritual rest found for God's people in His Messiah. The Sabbath pointed to God's work of purifying His people. In Exodus, God told them, "Above all you shall keep my Sabbaths, for this is a sign between me and you throughout your generations, that you may know that I, the LORD, sanctify you" (Exodus 31:13). The Sabbath was to be a sign that God sanctified them (made them holy). It was a lesson reinforced by their complete lack of work. As they did nothing, they were to remember that God had done all things needful for their salvation. His saving work, not theirs, is what mattered. The New Testament reveals that this culminated in God's Son, who completed God's saving work and gave God's people true rest for their souls. "The Sabbath was made for man, not man for the Sabbath. So the Son of Man is lord even of the Sabbath" (Mark 2:27–28).

The early Christians abandoned the old Sabbath laws. Their day of worship moved from Saturday to Sunday as a commemoration of Christ's resurrection and the new creation. Strict laws forbidding any kind of work were dropped. The focus was no longer on the lack of physical labor, but on the rest Christians had within their souls because of Jesus' labors for them. St. Paul taught the Colossians, "Therefore let no one pass judgment on you in questions of food and drink, or with regard to a festival or a new moon or a Sabbath. These are a shadow of the things to come, but the substance belongs to Christ" (Colossians 2:16–17). Sabbaths, festivals, laws about food, and other ceremonial laws were "shadows of things to come." Their purpose was to point to the Messiah. When the reality of God's Son entered the world and fulfilled God's will, the old symbols were no longer needed. So St. Paul tells the Christians in Colossae that they are not bound by the old ceremonial laws because the substance is in Christ.

At another point, certain Jewish converts objected that circumcision laws were not being followed by the new Gentile converts to Christianity. St. Paul's answer to their concern was "For in Christ Jesus neither circumcision nor un-circumcision counts for anything, but only faith working through love" (Galatians 5:6). Christ changed the relationship of God's people to ceremonials laws. What mattered was Jesus' fulfillment of the law and the genuineness of faith given through grace, not the individual's outward keeping of ceremonial laws.

CIVIL LAW

Civil law is similar to ceremonial law in that it was time-bound. It was meant only for the Old Testament Israelite community. Examples of these laws include laws about lending and not charging interest, voluntary and involuntary manslaughter, recompense for property damage, laws having to do with harvest and leaving certain parts of a field un-harvested for the poor to glean, and laws on marriage and remarriage in the case of the death of a husband without children.[4] These laws were

---

[4] A series of civil laws and corresponding punishments can be found in Exodus 21. It should be noted that Gerhard recognized that the distinction between some ceremonial and civil laws is unclear, so that scholars place certain rules in different categories (Gerhard, *On the Law of God*, 277).

understood as obligations for all Jews, not as general laws governing the whole of humanity.[5]

There are points where Old Testament civil and moral law intersected. Civil law dictated certain punishments for certain crimes. Sometimes these crimes included moral violations such as stealing, murder, and adultery. Yet these civil punishments, which were prescribed for Old Testament violations, were not carried over into the apostolic teaching for New Testament Christians. Prohibitions for moral offenses remained, but the civil punishments were no longer part of their instruction. Violations for civil and moral laws were left to civil authorities to administer. It was not the duty of the church to define or enforce civil laws.

MORAL LAW

The third division of law in the Bible is moral law. Moral law does not deal with Jewish worship rituals, as did ceremonial law, or with laws and penalties for Jewish society. It deals with one's behavior and even thoughts on a daily basis.[6] Moral law is understood as applicable to all human beings, not just to the Jews. Its repetition and broad application in both testaments shows that it transcends time and culture.[7] Examples of moral law include laws forbidding stealing, murder, coveting, and adultery, and laws that prescribe helping the poor and being fair and truthful. As it concerns the topic of sexuality, it must be noted that commands about marital fidelity, male/female relationships, promiscuity, and homosexuality are repeated in both Old and New Testaments and are applied to all people.[8] Laws governing sexual behavior are not time-bound or culture-bound. They do not change with location or social progress. They are properly characterized as moral laws.

The answer to the young man's question about why I eat shellfish and yet insist homosexuality is wrong is that the laws of eating certain foods belong to the ceremonial law, which is no longer applicable in the

---

[5] Chemnitz states it more strongly: "With the coming of Christ they (civil laws) were abrogated, so that they could be entirely omitted and that they might be rendered extinct" (*Loci Theologici*, 347).

[6] Gerhard, *On the Law of God*, 232.

[7] Chemnitz, *Loci Theologici*, 351.

[8] The basic principles of right and wrong with regard to sexual behavior mentioned in Leviticus 20:10ff. remain in effect in the New Testament minus the prescribed civil punishment. Cf. 1 Corinthians 5:1–8; 6:13–20; Galatians 5:19; Ephesians 5:1–7.

New Testament era. Laws regarding homosexuality belong to the moral law, which is applicable to all people. Jesus' example shows an understanding of the moral law continuing into the New Testament era. One might even argue that His application of certain moral laws was stricter than prevailing practice.

> Therefore whoever relaxes one of the least of these commandments and teaches others to do the same will be called least in the kingdom of heaven. . . .
>
> You have heard that it was said to those of old, "You shall not murder; and whoever murders will be liable to judgment." But I say to you that everyone who is angry with his brother will be liable to judgment. . . .
>
> You have heard that it was said, "You shall not commit adultery." But I say to you that everyone who looks at a woman with lustful intent has already committed adultery with her in his heart. . . .
>
> It was also said, "Whoever divorces his wife, let him give her a certificate of divorce." But I say to you that everyone who divorces his wife, except on the ground of sexual immorality, makes her commit adultery, and whoever marries a divorced woman commits adultery. (Matthew 5:19–32)

Jesus repeats and applies these moral laws of the Old Testament to the people of His era. Christians and non-Christians, Jews and Gentiles, remain under God's basic moral code. In the eyes of God, it is wrong in every culture and at every time to murder, to steal, and to be adulterous. Even those who do not know God's written moral code still have the moral law within their conscience. Paul teaches the Romans,

> For when Gentiles, who do not have the law, by nature do what the law requires, they are a law to themselves, even though they do not have the law. They show that the work of the law is written on their hearts, while their conscience also bears witness, and their conflicting thoughts accuse or even excuse them. (Romans 2:14–15)

Yet, even here within the far reaching moral law, the coming of Jesus changes things. The relationship Christians have to the moral law is different than that of non-Christians. Jesus has fulfilled the entire law for His people so that they will not be condemned for their violations of God's moral law. Paul told the Romans, "For Christ is the end of the law for righteousness to everyone who believes" (Romans 10:4). He told the Galatians, "Christ redeemed us from the curse of the law by becoming a curse for us—for it is written, 'Cursed is everyone who is hanged on a tree'" (Galatians 3:13). He told the Ephesians, that Jesus "has broken down in his flesh the dividing wall of hostility by abolishing the law of commandments expressed in ordinances" (Ephesians 2:14–15). To the Philippians, Paul explained that he wished to "be found in him [Jesus], not having a righteousness of my own that comes from the law, but that which comes through faith in Christ, the righteousness from God that depends on faith" (Philippians 3:9). This was a major point in Paul's teaching to every congregation where he ministered. Jesus was the fulfillment of the law for His people, so that even though they violated God's moral law and were deserving of condemnation, Jesus took their law-breaking into His own flesh and endured the punishment their law-breaking deserved.

That act of substitution protects Christians from having to answer for their crimes against God's moral law, and it does more. It changes how and why Christians follow the moral law.

Christians obey God because they are made one with Jesus through His forgiving gifts. Their obedience does not come from a sense of "having to obey or else," nor do they obey to earn God's favor or to gain a place in heaven. As Paul told the Galatians, "We know that a person is not justified by works of the law but through faith in Jesus Christ, so we also have believed in Christ Jesus, in order to be justified by faith in Christ and not by works of the law, because by works of the law no one will be justified" (Galatians 2:16). The obedience of Christians is not even necessarily a conscious act of doing. It is more a matter of faith naturally expressing itself.[9] Christians do what they do because Christ lives in them

---

[9] This is the view of sanctification expressed in the formative documents of the Lutheran Church. Cf. McCain, *Concordia: the Lutheran Confessions*, [Formula of Concord, Solid Declaration, Art. II, 63–64], 531. "When a person has been converted, and is thus enlightened, and his will is renewed, then a person wants to do what is good (so far as he is regenerate or a new man). Then that person will 'delight in the law of God, in [his] inner being' (Romans 7:22) and from that time forward does good to such an extent and as long as he is moved by God's Spirit, as Paul says [in Romans 8:14], 'For all who are led by the Spirit of God are sons of God.' This moving by the Holy Spirit is not a coercion. The converted person does good spontaneously."

and expresses His love and His obedience through them. Granted, they do not obey perfectly. Christians need constant forgiveness and renewal of their union with Christ. This is why the Church is so important in the life of faithful Christians. It is there, through Jesus' operation in His Word and Sacraments, that He restores His gracious presence and gives pardon for our moral failing.

It has been rightly said that there are only two religions on earth. One is a religion of law, where people seek the blessing of their god through various acts of obedience or devotion. The other is the religion of the Gospel where the blessing of God is given because of the obedience of another (Jesus) on behalf of the believer. The moral law is not seen by Christians as their path to win the love of God. That love has been won through Jesus' perfect obedience on behalf of imperfect people. The moral law is, however, the way that Christians express the love of God to the world through their daily dealings with other people.

Christian failure to accept homosexuality is linked to racial prejudice

The argument here is that the present day Christian's opposition to homosexuality is an extension of an older Christian failure to accept racial equality. This argument is deeply entrenched in many of the people to whom I speak. They honestly believe that Christianity has been discriminatory with regard to race and that its opposition to homosexuality is just another example of an endemic problem. This is not a new argument; it dates back decades.[10] Race and sexual preference have been linked together by the earliest proponents of the sexual revolution in America. Nearly every time I present this topic to a secular audience, someone levels the charge that Christianity failed in the past when it came to racial discrimination and it is failing again today in the same way toward homosexuals.

There are several layers to this argument that need to be dissected. At the base of their accusation is the fundamental belief in sexual immutability. They believe that being homosexual is like being African, Caucasian, or Asian; it is something into which one is born; it is essential to one's personal being and cannot be altered. Race and sexual

---

[10] Socarides, *Homosexuality: A Freedom Too Far*, 59.

"orientation" are both cut from the same cloth and are morally neutral issues. Because it is immutable in the same way as race, homosexuality should therefore be considered a civil rights issue, not a moral issue, and should be protected by anti-discrimination laws. This argument has been used with great success through the court systems and is the ultimate reason behind the ruling of the United States Supreme Court. Immutability removes the charge of immorality and makes sexual preference a civil rights issue. Inevitably, those who have taken this line of reason, wind up blaming Christianity for slavery in America. Some go further and claim that it is not simply Christianity as a belief system that permitted slavery, but the Christian Bible itself that encouraged and promoted slavery. They say that the Bible is an instrument of oppression.

Answering the homosexual/racial argument must be done one layer at a time. I have already discussed the problems in the previous chapter with claiming sexual "orientation" is immutable. I will return to that topic in the next section when I discuss the argument that people are "born that way." To equate homosexuality with race as an immutable trait is to do an injustice to people who have endured genuine and profound suffering because of truly immutable characteristics like skin color or nationality of birth.

The accusation that Christianity failed to protect slaves in early America is a more difficult argument to defend. We must admit that there were Christians and even Christian churches who either were silent about slavery or who tried to use the Bible to justify slavery. Jefferson Davis, president of the Confederate states, is famously known to have said,

> It is enough for me elsewhere to know, that it [*slavery*] was established by decree of Almighty God, that it is sanctioned in the Bible, in both Testaments, from Genesis to Revelations [sic]; that it has existed in all ages; has been found among the people of the highest civilization, and in nations of the highest proficiency in the arts.[11]

There were slave owners and traders who claimed to be Christian. Without question, there are historical examples of pastors and churches

---

[11] As an example of the kind of rhetoric used during the age of slavery, see Dunbar Rowland, *Jefferson Davis, Constitutionalist; His Letters, Papers, and Speeches*, vol. 1 (Jackson MS: Mississippi Dept. of Archives and History, 1923), 286.

who should have spoken up about the immorality of slavery and did not.[12] Some may have been afraid to speak up for fear of persecution. Others might truly have been racists and did not see a problem with slavery. So, yes, certain Christians and churches failed to oppose slavery in early America, but that does not mean that Christianity itself failed. Nor does it mean that the failure of some people represents a fundamental error in Scripture. Human beings sin. Churches filled with human beings can also sin individually and collectively. Those churches, pastors, and Christians who either were silent or promoted slavery did so in violation of the law of Christian love and the moral command to protect the weak (Psalm 82:3–4; Isaiah 1:17; Zechariah 7:8–10; James 2:1–13).

To be fair historically, it should be noted that Christians did take leadership in the fight against slavery. As early as 1688, Quakers were publically protesting slavery.[13] The first Abolition Society established in America was founded by a Quaker minister. The Society for the Relief of Free Negroes Unlawfully Held in Bondage was established in Philadelphia in 1775 and led by Anthony Benezet. In 1787, the organization was given greater public recognition when Benjamin Franklin became its president.[14]

In 1839, Pope Gregory XVI issued the papal encyclical *In Supremo Apostolatus*. In it, he said,

> But as the law of the Gospel universally and earnestly enjoined a sincere charity towards all, and considering that Our Lord Jesus Christ had declared that He considered as done or refused to Himself everything kind and merciful done or refused to the small and needy, it naturally follows, not only that

---

[12] Orange Scott, *An Appeal to the Methodist Episcopal Church, Part I* (Boston: David H. Ela Printer and Publisher, 1838), 17. Here one might note the example of the Georgia Conference of the Methodist Episcopal Church, which passed the following resolution unanimously: "Whereas there is a clause in the Discipline of our Church which states that we are as much as ever convinced of the great evil of slavery; and whereas the said clause has been perverted by some, and used in such a manner as to produce the impression that the Methodist Episcopal Church believed slavery to be a moral evil, Therefore, Resolved, That it is the sense of the Georgia Annual Conference, that slavery as it exists in the United States, is not a moral evil."

[13] W. E. B. Du Bois, *The Suppression of the African Slave-Trade to the United States of American, 1638–1870* (New York: Cosimo Classics, 2007), 139.

[14] "1775 First American abolition society founded in Philadelphia," This Day in History, www.history.com/this-day-in-history/first-american-abolition-society-founded-in-philadelphia (accessed January 26, 2016).

Christians should regard as their brothers their slaves and, above all, their Christian slaves, but that they should be more inclined to set free those who merited it; which it was the custom to do chiefly upon the occasion of the Easter Feast as Gregory of Nyssa tells us. There were not lacking Christians, who, moved by an ardent charity "cast themselves into bondage in order to redeem others," many instances of which our predecessor, Clement I, of very holy memory, declares to have come to his knowledge.

We warn and adjure earnestly in the Lord faithful Christians of every condition that no one in the future dare to vex anyone, despoil him of his possessions, reduce to servitude, or lend aid and favour to those who give themselves up to these practices, or exercise that inhuman traffic by which the Blacks, as if they were not men but rather animals, having been brought into servitude, in no matter what way, are, without any distinction, in contempt of the rights of justice and humanity, bought, sold, and devoted sometimes to the hardest labour. Further, in the hope of gain, propositions of purchase being made to the first owners of the Blacks, dissensions and almost perpetual conflicts are aroused in these regions.

We reprove, then, by virtue of Our Apostolic Authority, all the practices above mentioned as absolutely unworthy of the Christian name. By the same Authority We prohibit and strictly forbid any Ecclesiastic or lay person from presuming to defend as permissible this traffic in Blacks under no matter what pretext or excuse, or from publishing or teaching in any manner whatsoever, in public or privately, opinions contrary to what We have set forth in this Apostolic Letter.[15]

---

[15] Pope Gregory XVI, *In Supremo Apostolatus* (Apostolic Letter condemning the slave trade read during the 4th Provincial Council of Baltimore), December 3, 1839. www.papalencyclicals.net/Greg16/g16sup.htm (accessed January 25, 2016).

The pope's encyclical would have influenced many Catholics in the U.S. at a crucial point in the abolition movement. It is believed that in 1840, there were some 600,000 Catholics in America.[16]

Harriet Beecher Stowe was the daughter of a Presbyterian minister. As a child, she listened to her father preach bold anti-slavery sermons calling on people to put their faith into action.[17] Her novel, *Uncle Tom's Cabin* (1852), became a major force in the public discourse about slavery and helped expose its immorality. Through the character of "the Doctor," Ms. Stowe presented her case as follows:

> "Did it never occur to you my friend," said the Doctor, "that the enslaving of the African race is a clear violation of the great law which commands us to love our neighbor as ourselves,— and a dishonor upon the Christian religion, more particularly in us Americans, whom the Lord hath so marvellously [sic] protected in our recent struggle for our own liberty?" Simeon started at the first words of this address, much as if some one [sic] had dashed a bucket of water on his head, and after that rose uneasily, walking the room and playing with the seals of his watch. "I—I never regarded it in this light," he said. "Possibly not, my friend," said the Doctor,—"so much doth established custom blind the minds of the best men."[18]

Uncle Tom's Cabin sold 10,000 copies in America its first week and 300,000 copies by its first year.[19] It helped sway public opinion against slavery by citing Christian morality and Scripture against it.

The actual history of Christian involvement with American slavery is complicated. There were people using the Bible to justify slavery, and there were people publicly opposing slavery with the same Bible. The argument claiming Christianity has a history of injustice is simply untrue. Certain people identifying as Christians were unjust, but many

---

[16] Tom Frascella, "Early US Catholics and Catholic Immigrants 1790–1850" March 2014, San Feles Society of New Jersey, www.sanfelesesocietynj.org/History%20Articles/Early_US_Catholics_and_immigrants_1790-1850.htm (accessed January 25, 2016).

[17] Harriet Beecher Stowe Center, "Beecher Family," www.harrietbeecherstowecenter.org/hbs/beecher_family.shtml (accessed January 25, 2016).

[18] Harriet Beecher Stowe, "The Minister's Wooing," *The Atlantic Monthly*, vol. 3, no. 18 (April, 1859): 507.

[19] Harriet Beecher Stowe Center, "Uncle Tom's Cabin," www.harrietbeecherstowecenter.org/utc/ (accessed January 25, 2016).

more Christians fought to end slavery because the Christian faith was not compatible with the practice of slavery in antebellum America.

Nor is it honest to claim that the Bible itself supports the cruel mistreatment of people as exhibited in American slavery. The Bible's relationship to slavery is not a simple one. It does permit slavery, but the character of what the Bible permits under the title *slavery* is something very different than American slavery. Once more, context determines meaning. In our American context, slavery conjures up images of the most inhumane and heartless treatment of human beings imaginable. Dogs were shown more compassion than people in some cases. Dignity was stripped away and slaves were seen as subhuman. Sadly, that kind of slavery is not isolated to American history. Slaves were treated without regard for their humanity throughout recorded history in most civilizations.

Slavery was a given in ancient times. Even the biblical patriarchs kept slaves, but their treatment of them was not like the treatment of American slaves. Abraham's manservant was treated with dignity as a member of his household and was entrusted with managing his home and with finding a wife for his son Isaac. Hagar, who was the mother of Abraham's son Ishmael, was Sarah's servant. Jacob's wives Rachel and Leah had female servants whom they gave to Isaac to bear children on their behalf. These "servants" represent a form of slavery, but their relationship to the patriarchs was not oppressive or cruel. Every indication is that they served their roles willingly and were treated more like members of the family than as chattel. As difficult as it is for us to understand now, slavery in biblical times was sometimes self-chosen. A person might choose servitude as a means of working off a debt, or it might simply be the way a person chose to earn his or her livelihood. This is sometimes called "indentured servitude."

This kind of "slavery" was not racially motivated. In Exodus 21:1ff., there are laws regarding Hebrew slaves serving Hebrew masters; slaves were not treated as sub-humans incapable of living free lives. The law granted them freedom after six years of service if they wanted it. Exodus 21 set the rule that slaves should be set free if their master beat them and caused them to lose an eye or a tooth. If a master killed a slave, he was to be punished. Though admittedly, if the slave lived for several days after a beating and then died, the master was not to be punished. There were practices in the Old Testament that are not in keeping with our modern American understanding of equality. But slaves were given protection under law and, in the example of the patriarchs, were treated respectfully. There is no evidence in the Bible of any Jewish patriarch claiming the Jewish race had the right to enslave other races or that masters had a divine right to treat their servants/slaves with cruelty.

In the New Testament, the word *slave* (Greek δοῦλος, *doulos*) is used to describe servitude among the Jews and New Testament Christians. Slavery was commonplace in the days of Christ and the apostles. In her book *Slavery in Early Christianity*, Jennifer Glancy writes:

> As Paul traveled from city to city, then he would have found it impossible to avoid contact with slaves. When he went to the marketplace to find other craftspeople or to purchase food for dinner he would have mingled with both male and female slaves. A wide variety of evidence attests to the ubiquitous presence of slaves in marketplaces. . . . The other shoppers he encounters in the marketplace would have included male and female slaves, freedmen and freedwomen, as well as freeborn folk of the lower economic strata. . . . Slaves could be found in every occupation in Greco-Roman cities. . . . Slaves worked in pottery factories and on farms, in mines and as shepherds. In smaller establishments a slave might have multiple jobs. . . . Evidence is extensive for the involvement of slaves in the production of commodities, where they typically worked alongside free laborers. . . . Slaves were ubiquitous in all ranks of garment workers, from weavers to dyers to seamstresses.
>
> Along with labor in workshops, fields, and markets, slaves advanced their owners' financial ends through serving as financial agents and managers of all kinds. Ostraca document the activities of slaves who served as financial agents, often with some autonomy.[20]

This is something different than the usual picture painted of American slaves chained in rows and prohibited from exercising basic freedoms. Slaves in biblical times were often treated more as servants and could actually work their way out of slavery to gain their freedom.

---

[20] Jennifer A. Glancy, *Slavery in Early Christianity* (Oxford: Oxford University Press, 2002), 42–43. © Oxford University Press.

It is true that the Bible does not explicitly issue divine commands to undo slavery as a social institution. Despite how many would try in our day to use the Bible as a declaration of social liberation for all oppressed peoples, the Bible is not primarily concerned with social reform. Its goal is salvation for all people regardless of their station in life. It is also true, however, that the Bible does encourage a view of equality in Christ that is incompatible with the social institution of slavery. In discussing the use of the word *doulos* (slave) in the New Testament, Kittle states:

> If slavery was not rejected from the Christian standpoint, every effort was made to bring it to an end. When a slave had the chance of freedom, he was to seize it joyfully, though recognizing that in the last analysis it made no difference whether he was bond or free (1 Cor. 7:21). More important, indeed, the only important factor, is the active and passive subordination of slaves also to the rule which fashions the life of the community. This is the rule of love, which is rooted in the fact that all members of the community stand in the same relationship to Christ and are thus untied on the same level in Him. It is obvious that this must finally lead to the abolition of slavery amongst Christians.[21]

The entire book of Philemon in the New Testament is devoted to the relationship between a "slave" and his "master." Philemon was a Christian slave owner. His slave, Onesimus, ran away from him and somehow managed to cross paths with St. Paul, who was imprisoned at the time. Onesimus converted to Christianity and told Paul of his escape from Philemon. Paul intervened and pleaded Onesimus's case with Philemon. He sought to restore the broken relationship between the two:

> I appeal to you for my child, Onesimus, whose father I became in my imprisonment.

> For this perhaps is why he was parted from you for a while, that you might have him back forever, no longer as a bondservant but more than a bondservant, as a beloved brother—especially to me, but how much more to you, both in

---

[21] Kittle, *Theological Dictionary of the New Testament*, 2:272.

the flesh and in the Lord. So if you consider me your partner, receive him as you would receive me.

Christ changes the relationship between slave and slave owner into a relationship of brotherhood. Paul expects Philemon, as a Christian, to treat Onesimus with respect and love. He also expects Philemon to forgive Onesimus if he wronged him in any way. Paul calls Onesimus the slave "my child" and refers to himself as Onesimus's father. The master/property model of slavery popular in early America is replaced with a brother to brother model. The Bible speaks throughout of equality of importance in the eyes of God and of a new form of brotherhood between people. It does not support or encourage forced slavery or racial discrimination. There simply is no biblical statement, explicit or implicit, that promotes the dehumanizing practice of forced slavery of any race or people. In fact, St. Paul tells the Galatians, "For in Christ Jesus you are all sons of God, through faith. For as many of you as were baptized into Christ have put on Christ. There is neither Jew nor Greek, there is neither slave nor free, there is no male and female, for you are all one in Christ Jesus" (Galatians 3:26–28).

The attempt of homosexual activism to claim injustice in the Bible and blame it for slavery is really an attempt to remove the Bible from the discussion of homosexuality. If they can prove that the Bible is an instrument of oppression that supports an inhuman practice like slavery, they can make the claim that it should not be heard on an issue like homosexuality. If it is wrong at one point, it cannot be trusted at any point. This view makes no attempt to understand the biblical context of slavery versus servitude, and it fails to acknowledge the different character that slavery is given among Christians. It is true that the Bible does not try to abolish the institution of slavery, but is it also true that it does redefine that institution among the followers of Christ so that slaves are not treated as property but as equals to their masters in the eyes of God.

born That way: chasing the evidence

It is a given among many people today that scientists have proven genetic causes for homosexuality. During one of my presentations, a young woman raised her hand and asked, "What about all the scientific research that has proven homosexuality is genetic?" I asked her what research she had in mind. She answered that she could not list any examples by memory but that they were laid out in her textbook, and she would be happy to send them to me to get me up to speed. Then she laughed, as did her friends sitting next to her, evidently amused that I did not know science had settled the question. Fortunately, I was prepared for her question.

Her belief is one I have heard many times. University students tell me they are taught in class that science has proven homosexuality is rooted in biology. Students believe their professors because, after all, the professor probably has a PhD and certainly would not teach something that was not true, or so they believe. None of the students I have spoken to have ever pressed their professor to name the study that has proven beyond all doubt that homosexuality is in fact a biological or genetic condition.

In the following pages, I will review some of the supposed evidence for biological causes for homosexuality. It will be shown that the "proof" for a genetic source of homosexuality is nonexistent. To be sure, there are genetic abnormalities that do happen. There are those born hermaphrodites or with hormonal imbalances or with other medical conditions that affect sexual development. But in such cases, the physical problem can be isolated and identified. Hard science can find proof that some element of biology is disordered. Treatments can be prescribed that will help individuals deal with the problem and maybe even reverse the effects. Other times, there is no cure. But "homosexuality" as a biological condition or a physiological variant has simply never been proven in any scientific study.

It should be noted that even if genetics is at the heart of homosexuality (of which there is no scientific proof), that does not dictate one's personal behavior or ethical choices. Even if a person has a genetic propensity for a sin like alcoholism, he or she still has the ability to choose not to drink. Genetics is not the determinative factor for the choices we make. That being said, the link between genetics and homosexuality has not been established even though there have been many attempts to do so. The studies listed below in the section headings have been touted at various times as the long-sought-after proof of a biological basis for homosexuality. Some texts still reference them as scientific evidence suggesting homosexuality is an immutable biological condition. It will be demonstrated that other reputable studies disproved their original claims.

SIMON LEVAY AND THE STUDY OF THE HUMAN BRAIN

In 1991, Simon LeVay conducted research on the brain looking for possible biological causes for homosexuality. He studied a portion of the brain called INAH (Interstitial Nuclei of the Anterior Hypothalamus). There are four of these INAH structures grouped together in the brain. LeVay's study included a total of forty-one cadavers, thirty-five males and six females. He attempted to identify which males were homosexual (nineteen) and which were heterosexual (sixteen). All those identified as homosexual died of complications related to AIDS, as had six of the men identified as heterosexual (presumably having contracted it from using dirty needles). The sexual orientation of the subjects was presumed. Their actual sexual history was not available.

LeVay measured the volumes of the various INAH regions and recorded that the INAH3 region was larger in heterosexual males than both heterosexual women and homosexual men. His findings have been interpreted as physiological proof that homosexual and heterosexual people have different brain structures from birth. What is often ignored is LeVay's own interpretation of his research. In an interview published by *Discover Magazine*, LeVay admitted that he did not prove homosexuality is rooted in, or caused by, genetic factors. He further rejected the claim that his work supports the "born that way" argument.[22] There was no element of his research that attempted to trace the differences within the INAH3 region to birth or fetal development. All his study suggested was that there appeared to be a physiological difference at this single point in the brain.

A similar study was conducted by William Byne in 2000 (published in 2001). He advanced LeVay's findings by noting that the volume difference between men and women in INAH3 was due to a difference in the number of neurons, not in their size or density. Byne also noted a smaller INAH 3 in homosexual males than heterosexual males. This was determined not to be the result of fewer neurons (as in the difference between men and women) but a difference in neuron density. The neurons in homosexual men were packed more tightly together.

Byne offered two possible explanations for the difference in neuronal density. The first, which he discounts as being unlikely, was experimental error, where the tissue samples for the homosexual men shrank during

---

[22] David Nimmons, "Sex and the Brain," *Discover,* March 1994, discovermagazine.com/1994/mar/sexandthebrain346 (accessed January 27, 2016).

tissue fixation. The second explanation, and the one he favored, was that neuropil is actually less within the INAH3 regions of the brain of those homosexuals he studied.[23] Neuropil is basically the stuff between the neuron cells in which the cells are imbedded. It is a network of various nerve fibers (axones, glial branches, and dendrites) and synapses. The male homosexual subjects studied exhibited less neuropil than heterosexual males.

Byne cited research that explained the loss of neuropil as being rooted in the developmental experiences of subjects after birth. Studies by Bhide and Bedi (1984) and Turner and Greenbough (1985) conclude that postnatal experience in animals has been shown to affect neuropil in certain regions of the brain. In other words, behavior and life experience affect neuropil. The smaller INAH3 in homosexual men is not a cause of homosexuality; Byne seems to favor the smaller INAH3 being the result of behavior and experience after birth.[24] Instead of the structure of the brain influencing behavior, behavior can actually influence the structure of the brain. What LeVay seems to have found is evidence that homosexual behavior actually alters the structure of the brain.

Bailey Pillard Study of Twins

If the root causes of homosexuality are genetic in nature, then people who are very similar genetically should have similar sexual "orientations." Even more, identical twins (monozygotic) should demonstrate identical "orientations." In 1991, J. Michael Bailey, a psychology professor at Northwestern University, and Richard Pillard, a professor of psychiatry at Boston University, co-authored a study of twins looking for evidence of a genetic link that might direct sexual orientation. If they could show that homosexuality was shared among identical twins at a significantly higher rate than among twins that were not identical (dizygotic), or among siblings who shared similar genes, then they believed they would be able to demonstrate a genetic link for homosexuality. If genes are behind homosexual identity, then one would also expect that the rate of homosexual preference among nonidentical twins would be

---

[23] William Byne, Stuart Tobet, Linda Mattiace, Mitchell Lasco, Eileen Kemether, Mark Edgar, Susan Morgello, Monte Buchsbaum, and Liesle Jones, "The Interstitial Nuclei of the Human Anterior Hypothalamus: An Investigation of Variation with Sex, Sexual Orientation, and HIV Status," *Hormones and Behavior* (September, 2001): 91.

[24] Byne, *Hormones and Behavior*, 91.

the same as between siblings in general since the age of siblings does not affect genetic similarity.

The Bailey-Pillard study of twins claimed to find evidence for genetic influences on homosexuality, though the results were not exactly as expected. If homosexually were wholly genetic, 100% of genetically identical twins should have shared homosexual "orientations." Their results showed that when one identical twin claimed to be homosexual, 52% (29 out of 56) of the time, the other twin would share homosexual "orientation." By comparison, they claimed that only 22% (12 out of 54) of nonidentical (dizygotic) twins shared homosexual "orientation" if one twin claimed it, and a ratio of 11% (6 out of 57) where adoptive brothers were both homosexual when one identified as homosexual. They claimed that the much greater ratio of homosexuality among identical twins demonstrated evidence of a genetic source for determining sexual orientation. They are not the only researchers who have come to that conclusion. In 2000, Kendler, Thornton, Gilman, and Kessler published a study in *The American Journal of Psychiatry* in which they claimed that among 31.6% of monozygotic twins, when one twin identified as non-heterosexual the other twin also identified as non-heterosexual.[25]

In 2002, a study published in the *American Journal of Sociology* reviewed the results of these earlier studies and came to radically different conclusions. The study by Bearman and Brückner, entitled "Opposite-Sex Twins and Adolescent Same-Sex Attraction," used a much larger sampling of twins and took notice of the methodological weaknesses in previous studies. For instance, in previous studies, both twins were not always interviewed to determine sexual preference. Often one twin spoke for the other and made assumptions on the other's sexuality. A study by Kirk, Bailey, and Martin in 1999 gives clinical evidence that non-heterosexual individuals are actually more likely than heterosexuals to label their heterosexual siblings as homosexual. So any procedure that involves questions to a homosexual sibling about his or her twin's sexual preference is suspect. They noted another important procedural

---

[25] Kenneth Kendler, Laura Thornton, Stephen Gilman, Ronald Kessler, "Sexual Orientation in a U.S. National Sample of Twin and Nontwin Sibling Pairs," *American Journal of Psychiatry* (Nov. 1, 2000): 1845. Out of 324 monozygotic twins studied, Kendler et al. found 19 pairs where one claimed to be non-heterosexual and of those only 6 were found where both twins were non-heterosexual. 31.6% sounds impressive until one considers that it involves only 6 pairs of twins out of a sample base of 324 pairs. Six pairs represents only 1.8% of the total sample, which is very similar to the overall rate of homosexuality among the general population.

weakness in previous twin studies claiming to find a genetic link for homosexuality. The twins used in those studies were volunteers. Yet, other studies prove that those who volunteer for studies on sexuality tend to be more educated and possess more liberal attitudes than those who do not volunteer. The Bearman and Brückner study, in contrast, was based on the National Longitudinal Study of Adolescent Health, which involved children from across the country from the seventh to the twelfth grades. It was not based on a small group of twins volunteering for a study on sexuality.

Where Bailey and Pillard claimed a 52% rate (and Kendler et al. 31.6%) of shared homosexuality between (male) identical twins when one of the two identified as homosexual, Bearman and Brückner found a 7.7% rate of concordance (both sharing the same sexual preference) among males and a 5.3% rate among females when one of the twins identified as homosexual. Their findings radically contradict Bailey and Pillard and strongly speak against a genetic source for homosexual preference. Bearman and Brückner stated that the large discrepancy from previous studies was due to methodological error in the sample base of those studies. Instead of random sampling, Bailey and Pillard recruited volunteers from gay publications, and instead of direct questioning about sexual preference, they accepted secondhand judgments from a twin about his or her co-twin. Despite the fact that the methods of Bailey and Pillard were biased in favor of their predetermined results (finding a genetic basis for homosexuality), they still failed to deliver the expected result that would have supported their assumptions.

The one remarkable find in the Bearman and Brückner study was that same-sex attraction (not same-sex behavior) rates are much higher among males in opposite gender twins (16.8%) than among their female counterparts or among any other sibling group. When an older brother is present in the family, same-sex attraction among the male opposite gender twin falls to 8.8%.[26] It begs the questions why same-sex attraction should be so high among male opposite gender twins and why the rates change so noticeably when an older male sibling is present.

The explanation points to parental/social influences in determining sexual preference. Parents with an older male child have well-established gender expectations. The toys, clothing, and room ornamentation are male-oriented. The older brother will himself encourage male-oriented

---

[26] Bearman and Brückner, *American Journal of Sociology*, 1196.

play with his younger brother. The gender expectations of the younger twin's immediate social context directs him toward clear male self-identification. In homes where opposite gender twins are first children, there may not yet be clear parental expectations or boundaries for either gender. Toys and clothing may be interchangeable between the two. Both children may be treated much the same without regard for gender differences. From the earliest years of identity formation, a male child might identify with some gender-specific things that are socially frowned upon and assigned to girls. As Bearman and Brückner point out, girls can wear boys' pants without stigma, but boys ought not wear girls' dresses. Statistics on girls who were "tomboys" in their youth show there is no more likelihood that they will adopt a homosexual preference than the general population.

Male children seem to be much more susceptible to the influence of gender specific socialization than girls. The evidence points strongly to sexual identity being rooted in the earliest stages of child development. Sexual identity is influenced greatly by nurture, not solely by nature. It must be pointed out that while this study deals mostly with the matter of same-sex attraction, this does not always equate into same-sex experience. In order for an attraction to become an experience, a host of social opportunities must come into play. While the study found rates of same-sex attraction in adolescent groups widely varying between 2.7% and 11.4%, the rate of actual homosexual experience was under 2%. It is clear evidence that though the mind might fantasize about forbidden sexual acts, individuals are still able to control their actions. Homosexual thoughts do not necessarily make a person homosexual in practice.

HAMER STUDY OF CHROMOSOME MARKERS FOR HOMOSEXUALITY AT Xq28

In July of 1993, *Science* magazine published a research article by Hamer, Hu, Magnuson, Hu, and Pattatucci entitled "A Linkage Between DNA Markers on the X Chromosome and Male Sexual Orientation." The study claimed to find evidence of a linkage between markers in the distal portion of Xq28 and homosexuality.[27] Hammer et al. stated their confidence in their linkage findings by suggesting a certainty of greater than

---

[27] Hamer, Hu, Magnuson, Hu, and Pattatucci, "A Linkage Between DNA Markers on the X Chromosome and Male Sexual Orientation," *Science* (July 16, 1993): 324.

99%.[28] Unfortunately for Dr. Hamer, the research in which he was so confident did not stand up to later attempts to replicate his findings. In April of 1999, *Science* ran two articles that cast doubts on Hamer's study. One article, entitled "Discovery of 'Gay Gene' Questioned," reported that two teams of researchers tried to verify Hamer's findings but could not. It cited a report given to the American Psychiatric Association that found only a statistically insignificant hint of a linkage for homosexuality with the Xq28 markers.[29]

The second article, "Male Homosexuality: Absence of Linkage to Microsatellite Markers at Xq28" by Rice, Anderson, Risch, and Ebers, concluded that their research could not find evidence of a gene that had any major effect on sexual orientation at the location Hamer claimed.[30] The authors of the study sought to duplicate the Hamer study by recruiting families with two or more gay children. To find them, they ran ads in gay publications. A total of fifty-two pairs of brothers were found who donated blood to be analyzed for the Xq28 markers (The Hamer study used forty pairs of brothers). The researchers did not find a remarkable pattern of shared markers at Xq28 that would have supported Hamer's findings.[31] The fact that more than twenty years have elapsed since the Hamer study, and no other research teams have been able to duplicate his results, effectively debunks his claim. Modern technology has not helped locate any genetic source for homosexuality.

Attempts to link homosexuality to some physiological cause are ongoing. New theories are being suggested linking homosexuality to hormonal levels within the womb during critical phases in a baby's development. Other studies have suggested that human pheromones might play a role in homosexual attraction. These theories are presented to students as given scientific fact (as evidenced by a conversation I had with a young lady who said this is what they taught her in her psychology classes at the University). But the real truth is that there is no scientific study that has definitively linked homosexuality to any physical cause. Science has not proven that "you are born that way."

---

[28] Hamer, Magnuson, and Pattatucci, *Science*, 325.

[29] Ingrid Wickelgren, "Discovery of 'Gay Gene' Questioned," *Science* (April 23, 1999): 571.

[30] George Rice, Carol Anderson, Neil Risch, and George Ebers, "Male Homosexuality: Absence of Linkage to Microsatellite Markers at Xq28," *Science* (April 23, 1999): 667.

[31] Wickelgren, *Science*, 571.

It must be reiterated that even if genetic or biological differences between heterosexual and homosexual individuals had been found, that, in and of itself, would not necessitate an individual living a non-heterosexual life. People still can choose to resist the urges of their flesh and follow a path of godliness. There are plenty of heterosexual people whose sexual urges push them to desire members of the opposite sex to whom they are not married. They can and, according to Christian teaching, should resist the urge to act upon those desires. Simply because one may have an urge that is biologically natural does not mean a person should act upon that urge. Self-denial is an integral part of what it means to be a human being and live in a civilized society. Every day people of every religion deny their natural urges. I would prefer to drive my car well over the speed limit to get from point A to B because to me, sitting in a car is a waste of time. But because of my commitment to God, government, and the other drivers on the road, I resist the urge and try to keep my speed within legally allowable limits. The fact that I have gotten only one speeding ticket during my thirty-five years of driving attests to the fact that I have been fairly successful keeping my urge to speed under control.

Whether our urge is one of self-preservation, anger, hunger, or of a sexual nature, we are not animals that immediately act upon our urges. God endowed humanity with the ability to resist urges that seem natural and choose a more moral path in keeping with His Word. I am in no way granting that homosexuality or any other sexual sin is in fact rooted in biology, genetics, or nature. The more researchers study homosexuality and try to justify it by hard science, the more they prove it is not encoded within some physical mechanism.

Sadly, the practice of many people today is to excuse virtually any behavior if it can be demonstrated (or even suggested) that it is rooted in nature. Recently, in a discussion about the grossly immoral life of Elagabalus, the Roman Caesar who competed with prostitutes for men and would stand naked in the doorway of his palace making purring noises at passersby inviting them to sodomize him, a young man brushed away his immorality by saying, "Clearly he was born with a desire for men, so his actions are justified." Apart from the fact that science does not support the premise that he or anyone else is born that way, that basic morality common to all human beings (not necessarily even Christian morality) should make clear that having sex with as many passersby as one can is deplorable behavior for any human being.

Why would someone choose to be homosexual?

I have had several people defend homosexuality by asking me why a person would willingly choose to adopt a lifestyle that invites persecution and discrimination. Homosexuality must, in their mind, not be a matter of choice but a matter of birth. It could not be choice because, as they see it, no one wants to face the kind of social stigma that homosexuality carries.

The underlying assumption that homosexuality brings conflict is not necessarily true anymore. There are certain situations where declaring oneself homosexual can prove beneficial. Basketball players who "come out of the closet" get phone calls from the president congratulating them on their bravery. Celebrities who announce they are homosexual get media exposure and win awards. Even on a less grandiose scale, being homosexual can qualify students for scholarships. As a parent who has put six kids in college, I have seen the list of scholarships available. There are scholarships open to LGBT (Lesbian, Gay, Bisexual, and Transgender) students and student activists. There are no corresponding "straight" scholarships; and should such a scholarship be offered, it would, no doubt, be rejected as discriminatory. Instead of inviting suffering, in the context of today's culture, homosexuality may invite preferential treatment.[32] The main thrust of the question is also terribly naïve. It assumes all choices are made through a reasoned weighing of options. But homosexuality is not always a matter of conscious choice. Further, people do choose patterns of behavior that bring suffering and misery into their lives all the time.

As discussed earlier, some people have their sexual identity damaged in early childhood through various forms of parental failure. Others are thrown into sexual chaos because of physical abuse, others because of emotional betrayal, and still more because of some other trauma. In such cases, the decision to become homosexual is not conscious or reasoned. The inner psyche deals with extreme distress by internalizing pain and

---

[32] For example, at Iowa State University near where I live, there is a special graduation ceremony for those who identify as homosexual known as the "Lavender Graduation." The ISU Lesbian Gay Bisexual Transgender Student Services website explains that the Lavender Graduation is way for the LGBTIQA+ community at Iowa State to recognize and honor their own. They claim over two hundred such graduates have been so honored over the past eighteen years (www.lgbtss.dso.iastate.edu/programs/lavgrad [accessed January 21, 2016]).

throwing that person's self-image into a conflicted state. There may be others who see themselves as homosexual who cannot identify any specific event or circumstance that accounts for their sexual preference. Perhaps it was part of early childhood socialization issues. I have met those who are homosexual by conscious choice. They were heterosexual but decided to experiment with sexual taboos, and after time, decided they enjoyed the excitement of rejecting social norms and engaging in homosexual acts. "Choice" is a very broad term that may or may not be within the conscious control of the one doing the choosing. The sad reality of human nature is that even if there are no traumatic circumstances forcing choices into a self-destructive path, people still choose paths that are harmful to them. Adam and Eve, who were in perfect harmony with God and had holy minds and holy thoughts, still made the choice to fight God's will and disobey Him. They chose to harm themselves.

Understanding that hiding deep within the same-sex attraction of certain individuals is a choice, whether conscious or unconscious, brought on by trauma, betrayal, abuse, or some other unknown mechanism, opens up the possibility of help. Those who want help with their same-sex attraction should be assured that help may be possible. Their unwanted homosexual tendencies are not encoded into their DNA. There may be avenues open through counseling or psychotherapy, or there may be help through the Church and its ministry. Even if the mind cannot be healed and people cannot rid themselves of unwanted thoughts completely, they may still find strength to face their temptations in the knowledge that Christ does not hate them and has died to ensure that even they have His power over sin at work in their lives. While many psychiatrists and psychologists in our day claim that efforts to "re-orient" homosexuals through counseling and therapy are "harmful" and never succeed, there are a good number of other professionals who disagree.

Success in treating people with homosexual desires has a long history. For example, in 1957, Edmund Bergler, a seasoned psychiatrist and author of numerous books on psychiatry, wrote *Homosexuality: Disease or Way of Life?* Bergler was an early pioneer in the therapeutic treatment of homosexuality. He claims to have counseled nearly five hundred people with homosexual tendencies.[33] His book discusses numerous examples of counseling sessions where the underlying psychological issues

---

[33] Edmund Bergler, *Homosexuality: Disease or Way of Life?* (New York: Hill and Wang Inc., 1957), 188.

behind a person's homosexuality are exposed. Bergler's opinion is that in many cases, there is an underlying clinical masochism that can be traced to conflicted issues with parents (particularly the mother) in early childhood. He relates situations where the mother was "smothering" or domineering, where her constant negative reinforcement led the child unconsciously to embrace suffering as a form of love. Similar problems arise with absent or abusive fathers, where the image of masculinity is one of failure and lack of love. Certainly, not all cases of children developing sexual identity problems come from bad parenting, but Bergler did believe that this may be a major contributing factor in many cases.

Bergler describes his therapy with homosexuals as requiring a great deal of time and self-searching. Sexual identity problems tend to be buried deeply in the subconscious. An adult may not even be aware of conflicted issues in his or her childhood. Bergler's experience with such therapy convinced him that psychiatric-psychoanalytic treatments over the course of two or three years could cure homosexuality, "provided the patient really wishes to change."[34] Some of his patients did not want to change and consequently were not helped by therapy.

Charles Socarides, another psychoanalyst who treated people with homosexual desires, supported Bergler's findings. He identified two kinds of homosexuals. The first chooses homosexuality consciously because of pressure from others or a desire to experiment sexually. This type wants to be homosexual and is not necessarily interested in changing. The second type, which he called "obligatory homosexuals" are people whose sexual identity was formed very early in childhood. They are people who have suffered in a variety of ways including sexual child abuse, emotional trauma, abusive parents, domineering mothers and neglectful fathers, abusive siblings, early exposure to adults engaging in sex, and many other traumatizing situations. Because their young minds did not know how to process their conflicted situations, they developed an inability to form relationships and/or generated feelings of attraction to the opposite sex. Socarides stated that males who are obligatory homosexuals are constantly searching to find their masculinity in others through "same-sex sex."[35] His book is truly an excellent book that addresses many issues relating to homosexuality and popular culture. He presents a convincing case that some people do unconsciously develop

---

[34] Bergler, *Homosexuality*, 188.
[35] Socarides, *Homosexuality A Freedom Too Far*, 17, 19.

homosexual identities that torment them and can be helped through therapy.

Today there are actually a good number of therapists who continue to help struggling homosexuals address the underlying issues behind their desires. Different psychiatrists and psychologists have different approaches and address developmental problems in different ways. In his book *Reparative Therapy of Male Homosexuality*, Joseph Nicolosi brings together many of the clinical causes cited for male homosexuality. His approach is compassionate, and he recognizes that not all homosexuals want to feel as they do.

> Some people define the whole person by his unwanted sexual behavior, based upon the simplistic phenomenological premise "You are what you do." In contrast, my clients experience their homosexual orientation and behavior as *at odds with who they really are*. For these men, their values, ethics, and traditions carry more weight in defining their personal identity than their sexual feelings.[36]

As previous therapists have found, Nicolosi believes that the drive toward same-sex attraction is rooted in early childhood. He believes that homosexuality in men is an alienation from males and he roots it in being "disenfranchised" by the father figure. Homosexuality in such cases represents a search for masculinity. "As Moberly (1983) explains, 'Homoerotic feelings must be reinterpreted as emerging for the legitimate need for same-sex intimacy.' But only through nonerotic intimacy will male bonding occur and masculine identity form."[37]

Along with the genuine hope of therapeutic help, the Christian who struggles with homosexual desires should be given the additional comfort that God gives grace and help to those who struggle. Within the worship of the Church, God gives grace upon grace to defeat guilt and shame. God speaks forgiveness over His people as they confess their sin and receive His absolution. Repentance and absolution do not mean the mind of the sinner is instantly healed so that no sinful desires will surface again. The flesh will fight with God's righteousness, but the nature of God's forgiveness is to pursue that which resists it. God connects His

---

[36] Joseph Nicolosi, *Reparative Therapy of Male Homosexuality: A New Clinical Approach* (New Jersey: Jason Aronson Inc., 1997), 13.

[37] Nicolosi, *Reparative Therapy of Male Homosexuality*, 21.

divine help even more intimately with His people through the Sacrament of the Lord's Supper. There He touches the corrupted flesh of His people with His own body and blood, promising further gifts of grace and His Holy Spirit. In the Church, God gives His people a community of fellow sinners who struggle with their own sins and who can give encouragement and support. Christ's redemption is a full and many-faceted thing that works on God's children from different angles, both to forgive and to strengthen for a holier life.

The apa decided homosexuality was not a mental disorder in 1973

The Diagnostic and Statistical Manual of Mental Disorders (hereafter DSM) compiled by the American Psychiatric Association did remove homosexuality from the list of mental disorders in 1973. Those supporting homosexuality cite this as a huge victory for their cause and as verification that homosexuality is as "normal" as heterosexuality.

The decision was not reached by new studies that proved the normalcy of homosexuality. It was a decision made under fire through threats and intimidation by radical homosexual groups. Charles Socarides was a witness to the events that surrounded that 1973 decision. He described what tactics were used by homosexual lobbyists to secure the change in the 1973 DSM.

> In 1970, gay activists made the first systematic effort to disrupt the annual meetings of the APA by flocking in to our sessions in San Francisco. In a panel on transsexualism and homosexuality, they denounced my colleague, Irving Bieber, and showered his presentation with derisive laughter. One protester called him "a mother*!#." Bieber took this very hard.

> Gays demanded a spot on the official program of our next annual meeting, in May 1971, in Washington, D.C. Otherwise, they threatened to break up the whole convention with their own terrorist tactics. Our 1971 program chairman, John Ewing, quickly agreed. That told gay activists they could get what they wanted from "the shrinks" by using calculated violence and threats. Sure enough, when the 1971 convention rolled around, gays stormed the podium during a solemn

Convocation of Fellows. Frank Kameny, who was always a key strategist in the whole thing, grabbed a microphone and issued a manifesto. "Psychiatry is the enemy incarnate. Psychiatry has waged a relentless war of extermination against us. You may take this as a declaration of war against you." He demanded that gays be allowed put on their own presentation.[38]

After several years of intense pressure, members of the APA leadership yielded to the demands of the militant homosexual groups. They agreed that not all homosexuals were mentally or emotionally harmed by their "orientation," nor did their homosexuality keep them from being fully integrated into society. When enough support for this new position was achieved within the APA leadership, the change was made to the DSM.

Socarides quotes a letter written by Nicolosi to the chairman of the Nomenclature Committee of the APA, the committee that established the change in language:

> In the history of psychiatry, has a heterosexual ever sought treatment for distress about his heterosexuality and wished to become homosexual? When I put that question in correspondence to the chairman of the DSM Nomenclature Committee, Robert L. Spitzer, he replied, "The answer, as you suspected, is no." Why does the profession no longer consider homosexuality a problem?[39]

A large body of psychiatrists, psychologists, and psychoanalysts did not agree with the change of classification for homosexuality and continued to treat it as a mental disorder. Eventually some of them formed NARTH (National Association for Research & Therapy of Homosexuality). They continue to offer treatment to those who are troubled by their same-sex attraction. Proponents of gay rights insist that such efforts only harm homosexuals and never succeed. But such claims are propaganda. The unvarnished truth is that therapy does help some people.

It is important to note that there were no new scientific studies that proved homosexuality was not a mental disorder. Had it not been for the

---

[38] Socarides, *Homosexuality A Freedom Too Far*, 160–161. Cf. Jeffrey B. Satinover, "How the Mental Health Associations Misrepresent Science" in *Why Not Same-Sex Marriage,* by Daniel Heimbach (Sisters, OR: Trusted Books, 2014), 407–413.

[39] Socarides, *Homosexuality A Freedom Too Far*, 9.

terrorist tactics of the homosexual lobbyists that overwhelmed the meetings of the APA and made many members of the psychiatric community
live in fear, the change to the manual might not have happened. To move
as quickly as possible to end the terror attacks on the meetings and on
individuals, leaders within the APA bypassed appropriate committees
and ignored volumes of scholarship that demonstrated connections between homosexuality and increased mental disorders.[40] Research showing the success of therapy in the treatment of homosexuality was dis-
missed. Members who disagreed and sought open debate on the issue
were silenced; therefore no open scholarly debate on the issue occurred.
Backroom politics won the day.[41] A more extensive treatment of the historical circumstances surrounding the APA's decision can be found in
Homosexuality and American Psychiatry: The Politics of Diagnosis by
Ronald Bayer.[42]

Those who claim a victory at the APA's removal of homosexuality
from their manual also often fail to mention that a new category of mental disorder was added to the manual. Quoting Ronald Bayer:

> On a final poll, with a vote of thirteen to zero and two absten-
> tions, the board approved the deletion of homosexuality and its
> replacement with the classification "sexual orientation disturb-
> ance" [*quoting the board*]. This category is for individuals
> whose sexual interests are directed primarily toward people of
> the same sex and who are either disturbed by, in conflict with,
> or wish to change their sexual orientation. This diagnostic cat-
> egory is distinguished from homosexuality, which by itself does
> not necessarily constitute a psychiatric disorder.[43]

The difference between the new category and old is that the category
of "sexual orientation disturbance" recognizes that there are some homosexuals who are genuinely disturbed by their sexuality and who want
help, while also acknowledging that other homosexuals are not bothered
by their identity and have no desire to get help. Not surprisingly,

---

[40] A number of these studies that were ignored are listed by Jeffery Satinover, "How the
Mental Health Associations Misrepresent Science" in *Why Not Same-Sex Marriage,* 422–
424.

[41] Cf. Socarides, *Homosexuality A Freedom Too Far,* 157–182.

[42] Ronal Bayer, *Homosexuality and American Psychiatry: The Politics of Diagnosis,*
(Princeton, New Jersey: Princeton University Press, 1987).

[43] Bayer, *Homosexuality and American Psychiatry,* 137.

homosexual advocates were not entirely happy with the new category. They wanted blanket acknowledgment that all homosexuality was normal. The APA's decision did not give them that. Bayer noted that Alfred Freedman, the president of the APA, stated that deleting homosexuality from the list of disorders in the DSM-II was not intended to be a statement suggesting homosexuality was normal, nor was it meant to suggest that homosexuality was as desirable as heterosexuality.[44]

The next edition of the DSM changed the language yet again to placate the pro-homosexual lobby. In DSM-III 1980 edition, the category of "Sexual Orientation Disturbance" was replaced with "Ego-Dystonic Homosexuality." Robert Spitzer, who was on the Nomenclature Committee of the APA in 1973 and helped bring about the change in classification, commented on how the new classification in DSM-III was received by the activists who pressed for change in 1973.

> (As Frank Kammeny, a gay activist, remarked to me in 1973, he had no objection to the category of sexual orientation disturbance, since any homosexual who was distressed at being homosexual was clearly "crazy" and in need of treatment by a gay counselor to get rid of societally induced homophobia.) Whereas in 1973 I was viewed by many as a radical who had joined forces with "gay lib," now, because of my defense of the DSM-III category I had become a reactionary betraying my own homophobia. Once again, it was charged (although now by those who regarded homosexuality as merely a normal variant) that politics had triumphed over science.[45]

The new category of Ego-Dystonic Homosexuality allows for recognition that not all people are comfortable with their same-sex attractions. It is recognition of a real-life conflict within certain individuals. Spitzer acknowledged as much, granting that the DSM-III recognized certain cases where a therapist should help his or her patient move away from being comfortable with homosexuality; helping some individuals estab-

[44] Bayer, *Homosexuality and American Psychiatry*, 138.
[45] Robert L. Spitzer, "The Diagnostic Status of Homosexuality in DSM-III: A Reformulation of the Issues," in *Scientific Controversies: Case Studies in the Resolution and Closure of Disputes in Science and Technology*, ed. H. Tristram Engelhardt Jr. and Arthur L. Caplan (New York: Cambridge University Press, 1987), 402.

lish sexual habits that are more acceptable to their sense of normality.[46] Even though the new language was an honest acknowledgment of genuine psychological dysfunction in some individuals, the homosexual lobby refused to accept it. So in later additions of DSM-III, the language was completely removed. By the time DSM-IV was published, the only mention of possible psychological dysfunction that would include homosexuality (without specifically mentioning it) was under the category, "Sexual Disorder Not Otherwise Specified." Point 3 of this category is "Persistent and marked distress about sexual orientation."[47]

The manual goes out of its way to avoid referencing homosexuality as a problem. Even as the manual identifies the diagnosis of "Transvestic Fetishism," marked by men who cross-dress for sexual purposes, it limits this category to heterosexual or bisexual men.[48] Homosexuals are excluded from the category involving cross-dressing! And yet, the manual recognizes that cross-dressing for sexual excitement is a pathological condition for those of other "orientations."

What the ever-changing DSM demonstrates is not advancement in science that validates the normalcy of homosexuality. Instead the DSM represents an attempt to placate ever-changing social opinions to the point of ignoring or at least marginalizing homosexuals facing genuine conflict over their same-sex attraction. People who are deeply disturbed by their same-sex attraction and have suffered tremendous spiritual and psychological conflict because of it are simply ignored. The goal of refusing to acknowledge those who are genuinely conflicted because of same-sex attraction is to deny their existence. The pro-homosexual community does not want to grant the possibility that homosexual attraction causes conflict within certain people.

"but the bible says you should not judge"

This is a statement I hear more from Christians than from non-Christians. It has the advantage of being biblically true. Jesus Himself does, in fact, say we should not judge.

---

[46] Robert L. Spitzer, "The Diagnostic Status of Homosexuality in DSM-III: A Reformulation of the Issues," *American Journal of Psychiatry* (February 1981): 213.

[47] *Diagnostic and Statistical Manual of Mental Disorders*, 4th ed., Text Revision (Washington, DC: American Psychiatric Association, 2000), 582.

[48] *Diagnostic and Statistical Manual of Mental Disorders*, 4th ed., 580.

Judge not, that you be not judged. For with the judgment you pronounce you will be judged, and with the measure you use it will be measured to you. Why do you see the speck that is in your brother's eye, but do not notice the log that is in your own eye? Or how can you say to your brother, "Let me take the speck out of your eye," when there is the log in your own eye? You hypocrite, first take the log out of your own eye, and then you will see clearly to take the speck out of your brother's eye. (Matthew 7:1–5)

There are also passages in James' and Paul's epistles that tell Christians not to judge (James 4:12; Romans 14:3–4, 10, 13; 1 Corinthians 4:5). Yet, as has been stressed repeatedly in this volume, sentences and phrases always fit into a larger context; and in order to understand the meaning of a word, phrase, or idea, the greater whole must be considered. The Bible has more to say on the topic of judgment than just "do not judge." For instance, St. John records Jesus telling a crowd, "Do not judge by appearances, but judge with right judgment" (John 7:24; cf. 1 Corinthians 6:1–3; 14:29).

When the Bible says "Do not judge," it is not forbidding Christians from discerning between right or wrong. The very nature of the Christian life requires constant assessment of right and wrong. Psalm 34 tells God's people to "turn away from evil and do good" (v. 14). In 1 Thessalonians, Paul says, "Test everything; hold fast what is good. Abstain from every form of evil" (5:21–22). Discerning between good and evil, which is judging, is a Christian necessity. Jesus' words in Matthew 7:1 cannot mean that all judgment is wrong.

The passage from John 7:24 where Jesus says, "Do not judge by appearances, but judge with right judgment," explains that proper judgment excludes appearance. What color a person's hair or skin is; how he or she dresses; his or her personal hygiene, mannerisms, or cultural tastes all belong to the realm of appearance and therefore cannot be used to judge the inner thoughts or intents of individuals. "Right judgment" is not a matter of "looks-like-it" guesses. It does not involve feelings or personal opinions of individuals. "Right judgment" is the application of God's Word to situations that are known and can be verified.

"Right judgment" is not a personal judgment but a repeating of that which God has Himself judged. Christians are bound to the judgments and decisions of God's Word. In John 12, Jesus told a group of people,

"The one who rejects me and does not receive my words has a judge; the word that I have spoken will judge him on the last day" (v. 48). If God's Word says something is spiritually harmful and Christians refuse to repeat God's warning, then they are violating the will of God, endangering the people God wants to help, and placing their own eternal life in jeopardy.

> Whenever you hear a word from my mouth, you shall give them warning from me. If I say to the wicked, O wicked one, you shall surely die, and you do not speak to warn the wicked to turn from his way that wicked person shall die in his iniquity, but his blood I will require at your hand. But if you warn the wicked to turn from his way, and he does not turn from his way, that person shall die in his iniquity, but you will have delivered your soul. (Ezekiel 33:7–9)

Where God speaks clearly, Christians must speak clearly. Where God is silent, Christians must be silent. What Jesus and the rest of Scripture prohibit is passing personal judgments apart from God's Word or judging by appearance without having all the necessary information.

As a pastor who is called to be involved with the most intimate details of people's lives, I am often put in a position of judging between right and wrong. I try to approach every situation with an open mind and an ear willing to listen. I am not able to look into people's hearts and determine their motives. I make no judgments based on my personal opinion of individuals. What I try to do is sit down with people and talk to them face to face. They explain their issues to me; they tell me what they did and why they did it. I take them at their word unless it can be proven otherwise. Through the course of my discussions with them, if it comes out that they are guilty of breaking God's Word, then I have to act as God's mouthpiece and tell them that they are at odds with His will. There are no personal judgments made on their character or their motives, but it is necessary for the good of their souls to point them to judgments about their particular sin that God has already made in His Word.

In a way, it is good that Christians are reluctant to judge. Each person should be so aware of his or her own sinfulness that he or she is hesitant to point to the errors of others. This is at the heart of Jesus' statement in Matthew 7:3, "Why do you see the speck that is in your brother's eye, but do not notice the log that is in your own eye?" Each should be aware of his or her own status as a sinful human being in need of forgiveness. Only in such a spirit of humility should one address the sins of others. But this realization of one's personal sin should not become so paralyzing that he or she cannot speak God's Word to those who are straying from it.[49] Jesus concludes His statement in Matthew 7 by saying, "First take the log out of your own eye, and then you will see clearly to take the speck out of your brother's eye" (v. 5). Once there is genuine realization of one's own sinfulness and repentance for it, then one can properly speak to others about their sin.

In Corinth, the congregation refused to pass judgment on a case of incest within the congregation. Their reasons for doing so are not clearly stated. The text suggests that it might have been a misguided understanding of the Gospel. Instead of condemning the sin, they tolerated incest under the premise that Jesus forgives all sins. Paul writes:

> It is actually reported that there is sexual immorality among you, and of a kind that is not tolerated even among pagans, for a man has his father's wife. And you are arrogant! Ought you not rather to mourn? Let him who has done this be removed from among you. For though absent in body, I am present in spirit; and as if present, I have already pronounced judgment on the one who did such a thing. When you are assembled in the name of the Lord Jesus and my spirit is present, with the power of our Lord Jesus, you are to deliver this man to Satan for the destruction of the flesh, so that his spirit may be saved in the day of the Lord. Your boasting is not good. Do you not know that a little leaven leavens the whole lump? Cleanse out the old leaven that you may be a new lump, as you really are unleavened. (1 Corinthians 5:1–7)

Paul does not hesitate to judge the sin and call it an offense against God. He does not assume to judge the character of the people committing it; but the outward act, which was ongoing and unrepented, he did

---

[49] Cf. Kittle's examination of the word κρίνω (*krino*—to judge), *Theological Dictionary of the New Testament*, 3:939. "From the fact that God's judgment threatens man it is often deduced that no man has the right to judge another, Mt. 7:1f.; Jm. 4:11; R. 14:4, 10; 1 C. 4:5. This does not imply flabby indifference to that moral condition of others nor the blind renunciation of attempts at a true and serious appraisal of those with whom we have to live. What is unconditionally demanded is that such evaluations should be subject to the certainty that God's judgment falls also on those who judge, so that superiority, hardness, and blindness to one's own faults are excluded, and a readiness to forgive and to intercede is safeguarded."

not hesitate to judge with God's Word. Where the sin remained and a repentant life was rejected, the Gospel did not apply. In such a case, the law needed to do its work and convince the unrepentant people that they were angering God by wicked behavior and needed to stop.

When Christians call homosexuality a sin, they are not judging the character of individual people. They are not setting themselves up as better or less sinful. They are simply addressing a specific sin that God has defined as such. When guilty people are pointed to the judgment of God's Word regarding a sinful action or propensity, they are able to hear God's call to turn back to Christ and be forgiven. When Christians refuse to speak God's judgment and call homosexual behavior sin, they are harming the souls of those who need to be called to repentance. What they think is being nonjudgmental is, in reality, confirming people in their sin and preventing them from hearing the message that their souls need to hear.

There is a good and gracious goal in speaking God's Word of judgment against sin. Christians, keenly aware of their own broken condition, want to see all people whose lives are at odds with God be reconciled to God. But in order for there to be restoration of the sinner to God, there must be an initial recognition of sin. It can be and usually is emotionally painful. It requires a great deal of compassion and humility in the person who confronts the sin. But true love for souls compels Christians to be honest and not withhold the truth from those who are erring. God the Holy Spirit will and does work through His Word, even when that Word initially must speak of law and judgment.

Summary

Recognizing the arguments and rationale of those who challenge Christian sexual ethics takes work. It can be difficult to listen patiently as evidence is presented justifying sinfulness. But by hearing the evidence and acknowledging possible kernels of truth in their position, Christians can at least be shown to be reasonable. The ethics of chastity in Christ that Christians display need not be presented as some knee-jerk reaction against progress (as it is labeled by many), but as a thoughtful answer to contrary evidence. The Christian case has nothing to fear from listening to both hands clapping. Hard science, sociology, and history do not stand in opposition to Christian morality. If anything, a thoughtful consideration of the evidence supports the message of sexual chastity in Christ.

chapter 6

REASON IN DEFENSE
OF OPPOSITE-SEX MARRIAGE

A world that will not listen to the Word of God and that rejects the moral basis of previous generations is a world where there is little hope of maintaining traditional sexual values. As the debate over same-sex marriage went into the courts in state after state, it was obvious that traditional values no longer guided the courts. With the ruling of the Supreme Court in June of 2015, the legal debate over same-sex marriage is now all but over. Not only have the historic understandings of marriage lost, but as the opinions of the four dissenting judges have stated, a new area of judicial interference in society's morals has begun.[1] Despite the apparent hopelessness of the situation, we as Christians are under a divine obligation to continue to speak God's truth, but speaking God's truth is not just a matter of quoting Bible passages. The historic understanding of marriage as a lifelong bond between one man and one woman is not limited to biblical teaching. There is a strong case in favor of male/female marriage that can be drawn from natural law and reason.

---

[1] Obergefell v. Hodges No. 14–556 (U.S. June 26, 2015), 3. (Roberts dissenting), "The majority expressly disclaims judicial 'caution' and omits even a pretense of humility, openly relying on its desire to remake society according to its own 'new insight' into the 'nature of injustice.' *Ante,* at 11, 23. As a result, the Court invalidates the marriage laws of more than half the States and orders the transformation of a social institution that has formed the basis of human society for millennia, for the Kalahari Bushmen, and the Han Chinese, the Carthaginians and the Aztecs. Just who do we think we are?"

Certainly, Christians should not shy away from speaking God's Word and pointing to the new chastity that is found in Christ no matter how outnumbered they become. There will be those who grow tired of godless immorality and want to know what God's Word says. To them, Christians must proclaim the biblical message of Christ as Savior. A better life can be built through His saving Word. It is a life not merely ordered by more laws but a life reconciled to God through Christ's purifying grace. Yet, there will be many who shut down all discussion at the mere mention of Jesus. For them, it is necessary to build a case for traditional morality that does not involve God's Word.

An example of how suspiciously the secular world looks at anything that remotely resembles biblical teaching was seen in my home state of Iowa when its Supreme Court addressed same-sex marriage. In its decision to allow for same-sex marriage, the Iowa Supreme Court made special mention of how religious (Christian) arguments against same-sex marriage are invalid and will not enter into the court's decision.[2] It further stated that opposition to homosexual marriage is primarily a religious matter,[3] going so far as to claim that religious opposition to same-sex marriage is *the source* of civil opposition. By blaming religion for being the root source of opposition to same-sex marriage, the courts necessarily excluded valid secular arguments because, in their opinion, such arguments could be traced back to religious bias.

During one of my lectures, a young lady asked if I thought my views about sexuality should be the legal standard for the country in deciding issues like same-sex marriage. On the one hand, I had to say that I agree with my Lutheran heritage on the separation of church and state. I do not think my religious views should be forced on those who do not want to

---

[2] Varnum v. Brien, No. 07–1499, IA, 65 (April 2009). "This contrast of opinions in our society largely explains the absence of any religion-based rationale to test the constitutionality of Iowa's same-sex marriage ban. Our constitution does not permit any branch of government to resolve these types of religious debates and entrusts to courts the task of ensuring government avoids them. See Iowa Const. Art. I, § 3 ('The general assembly shall make no law respecting an establishment of religion')."

[3] Varnum v. Brien, No. 07–1499, IA, 64 (April 2009). "It is quite understandable that religiously motivated opposition to same-sex civil marriage shapes the basis for legal opposition to same-sex marriage, even if only indirectly. Religious objections to same-sex marriage are supported by thousands of years of tradition and biblical interpretation. 30 The belief that the 'sanctity of marriage' would be undermined by the inclusion of gay and lesbian couples bears a striking conceptual resemblance to the expressed secular rationale for maintaining the tradition of marriage as a union between dual-gender couples, but better identifies the source of the opposition."

receive them. Lutherans have always understood that God's Word and His saving Gospel should be offered unashamedly before the world but forced on no one. On the other hand, I had to say that my opinions are not limited to Christian teaching. A person need not consult any religious view to conclude that same-sex marriage is bad for society. So in that regard, I do think that traditional views on opposite-sex marriage should govern society, not because that position is Christian, but because that position is defensible apart from any specific religious belief.

Moral issues can, and indeed have been, addressed in American jurisprudence by appealing to reason and natural law. Natural law is law that is self-evident to all humanity. It transcends time and culture. We see the appeal to natural law in the defining documents of our country. The Declaration of Independence reads "We hold these truths to be self-evident, that all men are created equal, that they are endowed by their Creator with certain unalienable rights; that among these are life, liberty and the pursuit of happiness." "Self-evident" truths are those that are, or should be, reasonable to every human being. They are the heart of what natural law is all about and they form the foundation for our country's legal assumptions. Thomas Aquinas boiled the sum of natural law down to a root principle, namely, "Good is to be done and pursued, and evil is to be avoided."[4] This principle is the basic rule driving all human activity and interactions. It is a rule that does not require a source document or a religion to define. It simply is that way because human reason makes it obvious to everyone that people should live for good and not for evil.

This most basic of all human laws can and should be applied to human sexual conduct, especially to laws governing marriage and family. If one looks at the laws that govern marriage in most states, one will find rules about who can be married based on the assumption that those rules are good for society and avoid certain evils. In the State of Iowa, and I suspect in most states, rules governing marriage include:

a. One must be at least 18 years of age.

b. Someone can marry at age 16 or 17 only with the consent of a judge.

c. One cannot be closely related by blood or first cousins to the potential spouse.

---

[4] Thomas Aquinas, *Summa Theologiae*, vol. II—Part II, First Section, trans. Fathers of the English Dominican Province (New York: Cosimo, 2007), 1009.

    d.   Marriage cannot involve more than one partner.

    e.   A person getting married must be legally competent.

    f.   Couples must wait three days to get married after getting a marriage license.

Such rules exist because the state has a vested interest in promoting what is good for society and discouraging what is bad. Sound marriages are good for society. Unhealthy marriages harm society. It is right and valid even in a world that rejects the Christian God, even for those who worship no God, to question whether a certain human activity is good or bad for individuals and for society as a whole.

The justices of the United States Supreme Court who agreed with the majority opinion legalizing same-sex marriage evidently believe that same-sex marriage does contribute to the greater good of society. They justify their position with such conclusions as "the right to personal choice regarding marriage is inherently in the concept of individual autonomy,"[5] "the right to marry is fundamental because it supports a two-person union unlike any other in its importance to the committed individuals,"[6] "it safeguards children and families and thus draws meaning from related rights of childrearing, procreation, and education,"[7] and "marriage is a keystone of our social order."[8] Each of these indirectly flows from the natural law argument. The underlying assumption in each claim is that there are rights at play that serve the greater good and that are inherent to being human, rights that are recognized by the U.S. Constitution. So the right of personal choice, the right to be joined to another person of your own choosing in "marriage," and the right for children to live without stigmas regarding their parent's

---

[5] Obergefell v. Hodges No. 14–556 (U.S. June 26, 2015), 12.

[6] Obergefell v. Hodges No. 14–556 (U.S. June 26, 2015), 13.

[7] Obergefell v. Hodges No. 14–556 (U.S. June 26, 2015), 14. This point is especially revealing of the court's logic. This claim is made on page 15 that "By giving recognition and legal structure to their parents' relationship, marriage allows children 'to understand the integrity and closeness of their own family and its concord with other families in their community and in their daily lives.' . . . Without the recognition, stability, and predictability marriage offers, their children suffer the stigma of knowing their families are somehow lesser. . . . The marriage laws at issue here thus harm and humiliate the children of same-sex couples." The court refuses to consider that the stigma children may feel is not due to the fact that their same-sex parents cannot call their relationship "marriage," but that homosexuality is inherently immoral.

[8] Obergefell v. Hodges No. 14–556 (U.S. June 26, 2015), 16.

sexual choices are inherent rights, according to the court, are essential to every person, and therefore serve the greater good of all society. Justice Roberts notes the connection of the majority opinion to the natural law argument in his dissenting opinion,

> Stripped of its shiny rhetorical gloss the majority's argument is that the Due Process Clause gives same-sex couples a fundamental right to marry because it will be good for them and for society. If I were a legislator, I would certainly consider that view as a matter of social policy. But as a judge, I find the majority's position indefensibly as a matter of constitutional law.[9]

Same-sex marriage was legalized because the majority of this one panel of judges believes that it contributes to the greater good of society. Those Justices who dissented from the opinion did so because they believe that such natural law conclusions do not belong to courts to decide but to society as a whole.[10] Regardless, we are where we are as a country and must now answer those who claim same-sex marriage serves the greater good and avoids a greater evil.

financial considerations

The government has historically created laws and provided financial incentives for married couples because it recognizes that stable marriages are good for society. There are social security benefits to spouses, medical benefits, and tax breaks for married couples; there is time given away from work for family leave and certain inheritance rules favoring the surviving spouse. One could include medical decision making as a financial benefit because it costs time and money to determine who has authority in such circumstances if not the spouse.

The state has a large financial stake in supporting stable marriages. Why all the financial benefits for married couples? Because the state recognizes that the family is the basis of society and stable marriages are good for the state's welfare and economy. When marriages are unstable

---

[9] Obergefell v. Hodges No. 14–556 (U.S. June 26, 2015), 10 (Roberts dissenting).

[10] Obergefell v. Hodges No. 14–556 (U.S. June 26, 2015), 5 (Scalia dissenting). Scalia writes, "This is a naked judicial claim to legislative—indeed, super-legislative—power; a claim fundamentally at odds with our system of government. . . . A system of government that makes the People subordinate to a committee of nine unelected lawyers does not deserve to be called a democracy."

and break apart, the costs to society rise. Broken homes mean broken people who must turn to the court system for justice and to counselors for support. Productivity at work may (will) suffer; physical health may require medical attention. There is a cascade effect of issues individuals may face because of broken marriages, which cost not only the individuals involved but the society around them. If children are present in the marriage, the costs escalate dramatically. Unstable homes produce more unstable children who then require the intervention of social services, law enforcement, court systems, counselors, and government assistance. Studies done in Scandinavian countries have concluded that state spending increases as marriage culture declines.[11] In a book published by the Witherspoon Institute, it was reported,

> Estimates vary regarding the costs to the taxpayer of family breakdown, but they clearly run into the many billions of dollars. One Brookings study found that the retreat from marriage was associated with an increase of $229 billion in welfare expenditures from 1970 to 1996. Another study found that local, state, and federal governments spend $33 billion per year on the direct and indirect costs of divorce.[12]

Unstable families cost society billions of dollars—dollars that could be used by families to raise the standard of living or by local governments to build infrastructure or care for a thousand other needs. A natural law concern for the greater social good must ask if same-sex marriages are as stable and beneficial to families, and therefore to society, as traditional marriage.

The effects of family structure

The Witherspoon Institute's booklet, *Marriage and the Public Good: Ten Principles,* identifies four challenges to the stability of marriage. They are divorce, having children out of wedlock, cohabitation, and same-sex

---

[11] Sherif Girgis, "Real Marriage," *National Review Online,* April 5, 2011. www.nationalreview.com/article/263679/real-marriage-sherif-girgis (accessed February 4, 2016).

[12] Witherspoon Institute, *Marriage and the Public Good: Ten Principles* (Princeton, NJ: The Witherspoon Institute, 2008), 16. See www.parliament.nz/resource/0000240464 (accessed February 3, 2016).

marriage.[13] Each familial structure presents its own challenges to the overall good. And nowhere is the overall good to society more important than when it comes to raising children. Familial structures likely to raise children requiring the intervention of the state are structures that the state has a vested interest in avoiding. Independent studies have confirmed that the best, most stable structure for the raising of children is in a low-conflict marriage with both biological parents present.[14]

Within the traditional definition of marriage as a lifelong union between a man and a woman is the assumption of children. The wedded male and female pair has the potential, even the expectation, for procreation. The more stable an environment the state can provide for the raising of children, the more it secures its own future well-being. The raising of children by both biological parents is important because each gender brings different elements into the socialization of children. Two men or two women raising a child cannot bring what a man and woman together can.

> Mothers are more sensitive to the cries, words, and gestures of infants, toddlers, and adolescents and partly as a consequence, they are better at providing physical and emotional nurture to their children. . . . Fathers excel when it comes to providing discipline, ensuring safety, and challenging their children to embrace life's opportunities and confront life's difficulties.[15]

Children raised in stable homes, where mom and dad love each other despite their differences, are more apt to contribute positively to society. As noted traditional-marriage apologist Maggie Gallagher states, "The passionate desire of the child for his mother and father is not based on sex roles, or tasks performed, but on a desire to experience both male and female love, and to experience his own creation as an act of love by both

---

[13] Witherspoon Institute, *Marriage and the Public Good*, 18–19.

[14] Cf. Kristin Anderson Moore, Susan M. Jekielek, and Carol Emig, "Marriage from a Child's Perspective: How Does Family Structure Affect Children and What Can We Do about It?" *Child Trends Research Brief* (Washington DC: Child Trends Inc., June 2002), 6, www.childtrends.org/wp-content/uploads/2002/06/MarriageRB602.pdf (accessed January 29, 2016). See also, Mary Parke, "Are Married Parents Really Better for Children? What Research Says about the Effects of Family Structure on Child Well-Being" (Washington DC: Center for Law and Social Policy, May 2003), 6. This study equates the outcomes of children raised by same-sex parents with those of divorced heterosexual parents. files.eric.ed.gov/fulltext/ED476114.pdf (accessed February 4, 2016).

[15] Witherspoon Institute, *Marriage and the Public Good*, 12.

his parents."[16] "Same-sex marriage attacks the underlying logic of marriage which is rooted in the experience of reconciling two genders."[17] The bottom line is that children need the presence and loving interaction of both genders to understand how to relate to and with each gender. Where the dual gender dynamic of love is not present, children suffer and therefore society itself suffers.[18]

There is a war of words raging over studies on same-sex parenting. In 2005, the American Psychological Association (the same group shown earlier as being highly politically motivated) cited fifty-nine studies in a policy brief on homosexual parents, which it claimed showed that homosexual parents can raise children as effectively as biological parents.[19] Loren Marks, then professor at Louisiana State University, examined the studies and came to the conclusion that the APA's assertions were not as reliable as reported. Several procedural issues in the APA's studies were listed in his article; such as a lack of heterosexual comparison groups in twenty-six of the studies,[20] and reports that the "repeatedly selected representatives of same-sex parents have been 'small samples [of lesbians] that are predominantly White, well-educated [and] middle-class.' "[21] In thirteen of the thirty-three studies where comparisons were made with heterosexual parents, the heterosexual parent sample was of single mothers, not of homes with both biological parents.[22] The remaining twenty studies that purported to use heterosexual comparison groups failed to specify whether those heterosexual samples were of single, divorced, cohabitating, or two-parent homes.[23]

Marks took aim especially at the APA's claim that "not a single study has found children of lesbian or gay parents to be disadvantaged in any

---

[16] John Corvine and Maggie Gallagher, *Debating Same-Sex Marriage* (New York: Oxford University Press, 2012), 113. © Oxford University Press.

[17] Corvine and Gallagher, *Debating Same-Sex Marriage*, 147. © Oxford University Press.

[18] John Wooden, head coach of the UCLA men's basketball team from 1948–1975, is said to have made the very wise and insightful statement, "The best thing a father can do for his children is to love their mother."

[19] Cited in Loren Marks, "Same-sex Parenting and Children's Outcomes: A Closer Examination of the American Psychological Association's Brief on Lesbian and Gay Parenting," *Social Science Research*, 41, no. 4 (July 2012): 735.

[20] Marks, "Same-sex Parenting and Children's Outcomes," 739.

[21] Marks, "Same-sex Parenting and Children's Outcomes," 740.

[22] Marks, "Same-sex Parenting and Children's Outcomes," 740–41.

[23] Marks, "Same-sex Parenting and Children's Outcomes," 741.

significant respect relative to children of heterosexual parents." Marks noted,

> In the "Summary of Findings" section, the APA Brief references a study by Sarantakos (1996), but does so in a footnote that critiques the study (p. 6, Footnote 1). On page 40 of the APA Brief's annotated bibliography, a reference to the Sarantakos (1996) article is offered, but there is no summary of the study's findings, only a note reading "No abstract available." Upon closer examination, we find that the Sarantakos (1996) study is a comparative analysis of 58 children of heterosexual married parents, 58 children of heterosexual cohabiting couples, and 58 children living with homosexual couples that were all "matched according to socially significant criteria (e.g., age, number of children, education, occupation, and socioeconomic status)." The combined sample size (174) is the seventh-largest sample size of the 59 published studies listed in the APA Brief's "Summary of Research Findings on Lesbian and Gay Parenting." . . . However, the six studies with larger sample sizes were all adult self-report studies, making the Sarantakos combined sample the largest study (APA Brief, pp. 23–45) that examined children's developmental outcomes. Key findings of the Sarantakos study are summarized below. To contextualize these data, the numbers are based on a teacher rating-scale of performance "ranging from 1 (very low performance), through 5 (moderate performance) to 9 (very high performance)." Based on teacher (not parent) reports, Sarantakos found several significant differences between married families and homosexual families.

Language Achievement	Married 7.7, Cohabiting 6.8, Homosexual 5.5
Mathematics Achievement	Married 7.9, Cohabiting 7.0, Homosexual 5.5
Social Studies Achievement	Married 7.3, Cohabiting 7.0, Homosexual 7.6
Sport Interest/Involvement	Married 8.9, Cohabiting 8.3, Homosexual 5.9

Sociability/Popularity	Married 7.5, Cohabiting 6.5, Homosexual 5.0
School/Learning Attitude	Married 7.5, Cohabiting 6.8, Homosexual 6.5
Parent-School Relationships	Married 7.5, Cohabiting 6.0, Homosexual 5.0
Support with Homework	Married 7.0, Cohabiting 6.5, Homosexual 5.5
Parental Aspirations	Married 8.1, Cohabiting 7.4, Homosexual 6.5

Sarantakos concluded, "Overall, the study has shown that children of married couples are more likely to do well at school in academic and social terms, than children of cohabiting and homosexual couples."[24]

The evidence seems to point to an obvious conclusion: that the APA purposely ignored a major study because its findings were not in agreement with the narrative the APA wanted in its portrayal of homosexual parenting. They did this even though this study was the largest comparison study documenting children's educational outcomes of all fifty-nine studies, one of only six studies to use three comparison groups and "the most comprehensively triangulated study (four data sources) conducted on same-sex parenting."[25] Others have noted that only four of the fifty-nine studies cited by the APA met the APA's own standards for statistical reliability. But none of the fifty-nine studies compared a large, random, representative sample of lesbian, gay, or bisexual parents and their children with a large, random, representative sample of married biological parents and their children. In addition, a number of the studies were based on parents' interviews about their children's experience, not on interviews with the children themselves.

In July 2012, *Social Science Research* published a study by sociologist and associate professor at University of Texas at Austin, Mark Regnarus. Regnarus sought to redress some of the insufficiencies in previous studies

---

[24] Marks, "Same-sex Parenting and Children's Outcomes," 742.
[25] Marks, "Same-sex Parenting and Children's Outcomes," 743.

by providing a much larger statistical sampling (questioning over 15,000 American families). He interviewed the children (ages 18–39) in a random sampling of homes directly instead of asking parents about their children. The Regnarus sample included children raised by both biological parents, divorced parents, single parents, lesbian mothers, gay fathers, adopted parents, and step-parents. His study, which not surprisingly has drawn sharp criticism from supporters of same-sex marriage, demonstrated notable differences between the children of same-sex attracted parents and intact biological opposite-sex parents. For instance, the children who reported that their mother or father had been in a homosexual relationship were more than twice as likely to have been in therapy than children raised by both biological parents. Children whose mothers had been in a lesbian relationship were more than twice as likely to have contemplated suicide than children from intact biological parent families. Those children who said their fathers had been in a gay relationship were nearly five times as likely to have considered suicide. Children raised by mothers who had been in a lesbian relationship were more than twice as likely to be receiving public assistance as those raised by both biological parents. Those raised by fathers who had been in a homosexual relationship were more than three times as likely to be on public assistance. In short, numerous markers including issues such as premarital cohabitation, unemployment, sexual abuse by an adult, sexually transmitted infections, alcohol and marijuana use, and numbers of sexual partners showed elevated levels in children who were raised by a parent who had been in a homosexual relationship compared with those raised by both opposite-sex parents.[26]

The claim that there are no studies demonstrating that heterosexual marriage is better for children than homosexual unions is simply not true. The studies are there and the findings demonstrate a notable difference in favor of stable, loving heterosexual marriages. The reaction of many of those who advocate for homosexual rights is either to dismiss these studies, ignore their findings, vilify the people making the studies, or find some minor procedural point to excuse all the data as faulty. The Regnarus study is broad-based and procedurally sound. It agrees with

---

[26] Mark Regnarus, "How different are the adult children of parents who have same-sex relationships? Findings from the New Family Structures Study," *Social Science Research*, 41, no. 4 (2012): 761–762. www.markregnerus.com/uploads/4/0/6/5/4065759/regnerus_july_2012_ssr.pdf (accessed January 30, 2016).

many other studies that children raised in two-parent homes with both biological parents fare much better than in any other family structure.

Based on consideration of the natural law principle that good ought to be pursued and evil avoided, a substantial argument can be made that the best familial structure benefiting society as a whole is that of lifelong monogamous marriage between loving opposite-sex spouses. This is a conclusion that is well represented in legitimate studies, and it does not require a particular religious perspective. It is also a conclusion that reaches far beyond the issue of same-sex marriage. Any broken homes or high-stress family situations create instability in raising children and result in higher rates of troubled youth. Unstable families are bad for the children who internalize their familial conflict, and they are bad for society, which feels the effects of children acting out because of their inner conflicts.

moral Considerations

Secular sexual morals are guided by little more than vague concepts of consent and feel-good emotions. "Morality" is a dangerous topic because in today's climate all morality is subjective, determined only by the private experience of each individual. What is morally wrong to me may not be to you, and who is to judge which view is better, especially if God and His Word are automatically excluded from consideration? The natural law principle of pursuing good and avoiding evil does provide a basis for discussing moral decisions with those who do not accept the Bible or the Christian God. Actions that are intrinsically harmful to people are generally thought of as morally wrong by a majority. A case can be made that sexual promiscuity and sexually aberrant behavior are morally wrong because they hurt people. As a pastor with decades of experience, I have dealt with people suffering from the effects of their own promiscuity. I have seen the damage it does to families and married couples, to children, and to individuals whose conscience struggles with memories of past mistakes. Sexual promiscuity leaves a trail of broken people and regret. It also tends to go hand in hand with an attitude that sees people as objects for one's own sexual gratification and not as beings worthy of committed love.

Inherent in the institution of traditional marriage is the pledge of monogamy. Monogamy represents something more than a simple promise not to engage in sexual acts with other people. Sexual exclusivity implies total commitment to the other wherein all that one has and is belongs to the other and vice versa. It is going "all-in" and betting every-thing one has on an enduring life with the other. It is also a commitment to care for and provide for any offspring produced by that sexual union. Encouraging monogamy is in the state's best interests because it is good for society.

A view of sexuality that rejects monogamy is immoral because it di-vorces sex from the implied "all-in" commitment that monogamy carries. This is not just a problem for those who support same-sex marriage, it is a problem for heterosexuals who no longer see the need for marriage as an institution, and who replace marriage with cohabitation. Cohabitation does not carry the same public declaration of monogamy inherent in marriage. Nor does it carry the same legal responsibilities or penalties for breaking the union.

When the issue of monogamy is brought into the discussion of mar-riage, there is a noted difference between same-sex and heterosexual mar-riage. While most heterosexual relationships begin with an expectation of lasting monogamy, the same is not necessarily true for homosexual rela-tionships. Even where there may be initial expectations for exclusivity between homosexual couples, far fewer of those expectations are realized in the long term than with heterosexual unions. In 1984, a study was conducted by David McWhirter and Andrew Mattison that tracked the relationships of homosexual couples. They identified 114 couples who began their relationship with the expectation of monogamy. After five years, 107 of the couples had sexual partners outside of their relationship; the seven couples who had not broken their expectations of exclusivity had been together less than five years.[27]

A 2010 *New York Times* article entitled "Many Successful Gay Mar-riages Share an Open Secret" summarized a report by a study group at San Francisco State University. The report concludes that monogamy is not a main concern for many gay relationships.[28] However, jettisoning monogamy runs the risk of losing the battle for public acceptance by making homosexual sex appear "cheap." So, rather than concede that monogamy is not important in many gay relationships, some advocates

---

[27] David McWhirter and Andrew Mattison, *The Male Couple: How Relationships Develop* (Englewood Cliffs, NJ: Prentice-Hall Inc., 1984), 252–253.

[28] Scott James, "Many Successful Gay Marriages Share an Open Secret," *The New York Times*, Jan. 28, 2010. www.nytimes.com/2010/01/29/us/29sfmetro.html?_r=0 (accessed January 30, 2016).

of homosexual unions have redefined monogamy. They speak of monogamy as emotional exclusivity to another person, not necessarily sexual exclusivity.[29] Placing monogamy into the realm of emotions, rather than the act of intercourse, allows sex with multiple partners while maintaining the public claim of faithfulness. One simply has to have sex without becoming emotionally attached. There does not seem to be recognition that this kind of sex demeans people and turns them into objects to be used rather than individuals to be loved.

There are clear differences between how homosexual culture and heterosexual culture view monogamy and therefore marriage. The number one cause for divorce among heterosexual couples is lack of sexual fidelity. Monogamy is more than an expectation for heterosexual marriage; it is the linchpin for marriage. When that pin is pulled, heterosexual marriages fail, but a sizeable percentage of homosexuals get "married" without the same expectations. Proponents of same-sex marriage argue that both views can coexist without one harming the other. Why not just let gay couples redefine monogamy in emotional terms and live as they want and let heterosexuals live by their code of sexual monogamy? The problem is that two competing and opposite concepts of morality cannot coexist without one destroying the other. The more culture moves toward defining monogamy in terms of emotional but not sexual fidelity, the more marriages between men and women will suffer. Since it is within heterosexual marriage that children are produced and raised, non-monogamy will force more children to live in broken homes. Families, children, and therefore society itself is harmed if monogamy is redefined.

Proponents of "open" marriages, particularly within the homosexual community, claim that sexual openness is a positive practice that leads to a stronger marriage bond. Yet, claims that homosexual marriages are more enduring than heterosexual marriages are patently false. Norway, where same-sex "registered partnerships" (which are legally very similar to marriages) have been recognized since 1993, has been the subject of several studies on same-sex divorce rates. A study published in 2012 examined marriage and divorce records in Norway from 1993 to 2011, a period of eighteen years. The authors of the study expected to find results different from earlier studies, which reported a much higher rate of divorce among same-sex couples, particularly among same-sex female cou-

---

[29] Trevor A Hart and Danielle R. Schwartz, "Cognitive-Behavioral Erectile Dysfunction Treatment for Gay Men," *Cognitive and Behavioral Practice* 17 (2010): 70.

ples. The eighteen-year period for this study offered a much greater sample base than earlier studies, and the fact that such unions had been part of public policy for nearly two decades suggested fewer couples would be rushing into their legal bonds because of its novelty. To their surprise, results had not changed to a significant degree from the earlier studies. They found that from 1993 to 2011, divorce rates among male homosexual couples were 38% higher than heterosexual couples, and divorce rates among female homosexual couples were 128% higher than heterosexual couples.[30]

Once more, the evidence supports the position that the model of one man and one woman living in a stable monogamous union is the best model for society. No other family structure has proven to be as beneficial to the overall stability of the community. In fact, other models can be shown to create an increased burden on society.

An argument that roots the discussion in the greater good for society soundly favors traditional marriage. This provides Christians a way to engage the world around them without citing chapter and verse in the Bible. The problem with this approach is that it can and does degenerate into a battle of sociological studies, the results of which can be manipulated. In a Christian ethic, sociological studies can never replace the force of Holy Scripture. However, Christians can find support for traditional views of marriage and sexuality in secular evidence.

The painful truth of human nature is that facts and statistics do not win souls. I have had more than one frustrating conversation with individuals who admit there is ample evidence favoring traditional views on marriage and morality but who also say they do not care. Their hearts want to believe that homosexuality is acceptable to God, and He will not judge sexual immorality. And because they want to believe it, they dismiss any argument to the contrary no matter how logical or statistically verifiable it is. The natural law argument may provide an avenue for further discussion with the world, but in practical terms, it will probably sway very few.

One also sees well-intentioned Christians trying to appease both sides of the debate. Self-professed Christians have said, "While I'm not in agreement with homosexual marriage, what they do in private is their

---

[30] Kenneth Aarskaug Wiik, Ane Seierstad, and Turid Noack, "Divorce in Norwegian Same-Sex Marriages 1993–2011." Discussion Paper (Statistics Norway Research Department, No. 723, December 2012), 15. www.ssb.no/a/publikasjoner/pdf/DP/dp723.pdf (accessed January 30, 2016).

business and it does not affect me." They say this with the best of intentions, trying to maintain their religious opposition to practices that are contrary to God's Word while giving a nod to the world's expectation of tolerance. They are saying in effect, "I believe this way, but can tolerate that way." Yet, when tolerance allows the greater good to be suppressed and allows for practices that will harm people, then tolerance itself becomes bad. It is an essential element of any rule of law that lines need to be drawn where tolerance ends and the safety of others is protected. It is not unloving to say that this or that practice should not be tolerated by society because it is harmful. In fact, our society does that now with such practices as intercourse with animals, marrying blood relatives, polygamous marriage (for the time being), and ages of consent. Tolerance can become an excuse for lawlessness (including rejection of basic natural law principles) and failure to show love. When Jesus described to His disciples how corrupt the world would become prior to His return, He described this very scenario. He warned, "Because lawlessness will be increased, the love of many will grow cold" (Matthew 24:12).

The fallout

The effects of the collapse of traditional marriage are just beginning to be felt now because we are in the initial stages of it. As they manifest, they will prove pervasive throughout culture. The core understandings of what marriage is will erode. Instead of men and women entering marriage with the force of social expectation pushing them toward sexual monogamy, self-emptying love, and personal sacrifice to make the marriage last, they will enter their union with society's new vision of sexual permissiveness and the expectation that husbands and wives will seek themselves. Divorce rates will increase. Marriage itself will become irrelevant and couples will choose instead to cohabitate. Children will become less and less the focus of a couple's love and a reason for couples fully to commit to each other for life. They will become casualties because they are no longer seen as an essential outcome of the marriage bond.

There will be more consequences felt by anyone who dares to question the new cultural standards. As Maggie Gallagher put it,

> Equality is the state's religion in America. Ideas and people who are perceived as "anti-equality" do not get to play on a level playing field, but one decidedly tilted against their views

by government, law, and society. Equality arguments do not lead to pluralism but to the use of government and social power to suppress dissent, dissenters, and dissenting institutions.[31]

Already this is being felt by people who refuse to put their stamp of approval on same-sex marriage. Bakers are fined tens of thousands of dollars for refusing to participate in same-sex marriage celebrations.[32] County clerks are walking away from their jobs rather than be forced to issue marriage licenses to same-sex couples.[33] Teachers in secular schools are fired or suspended for stating their personal beliefs that homosexuality is wrong.[34] Such persecution will only increase, and sadly, the generations following us will feel the consequences more.[35]

---

[31] Corvine and Gallagher, *Debating Same-Sex Marriage*, 127. © Oxford University Press.

[32] Ben Johnson, "Oregon judge fines Christian bakers $135,000 for refusing to bake a gay 'wedding' cake," *Life Site News*, April 27, 2015. www.lifesitenews.com/news /oregon-judge-fines-christian-bakers-135000-for-refusing-to-bake-a-gay-weddi (accessed January 5, 2016).

[33] Three workers left their jobs in Decatur County, TN, rather than be forced to violate their conscience and issue same-sex marriage licenses. Cf. Nicole Hensley, "Entire Tennessee county clerk staff resigns over Supreme Court's gay marriage decision," *New York Daily News*, July 4, 2015. www.nydailynews.com/news/national/tenn-county-clerk-staff-resigns-gay-marriage-ruling-article-1.2281567 (accessed January 5, 2016).

[34] *Huffington Post UK*, "Robert Haye, Teacher Who Told Class Homosexuality Was 'Disgusting', Has Ban Upheld," December 4, 2013, www.huffingtonpost.co.uk/2013/04/12 /homophobic-teacher-robert-haye-ban-upheld_n_3067847.html (accessed January 5, 2016). See also the case of Ken Howell, adjunct professor at the University of Illinois, who was forced from his position for saying he agrees with Catholic teaching on the immorality of homosexuality. Kelly Salomon, "The Suppression of Christian Speech on American Campuses: Dr. Ken Howell's Story" in *Catholic Education Daily*, the Cardinal Newman Society, April 3, 2014, www.cardinalnewmansociety.org/CatholicEducationDaily /DetailsPage/tabid/102/ArticleID/3157/The-Suppression-of-Christian-Speech-on-American-Campuses-Dr-Ken-Howell%E2%80%99s-Story.aspx (accessed January 5, 2016).

[35] Obergefell v. Hodges No. 14–556 (U.S. June 26, 2015), (Alito dissenting). Alito warns of the future consequences of the court's decision, "As I wrote in Windsor: 'The family is an ancient and universal human institution. Family structure reflects the characteristics of a civilization, and changes in family structure and in the popular understanding of marriage and the family can have profound effects" (5). "The long-term consequences of this change are not now known and are unlikely to be ascertainable for some time to come" (5–6). "If a bare majority of Justices can invent a new right and impose that right on the rest of the country, the only real limit on what future majorities will be able to do is their own sense of what those with political power and cultural influence are willing to tolerate. Even enthusiastic supporters of same-sex marriage should worry about the scope of the power that today's majority claims" (7). "But all Americans, whatever their thinking on that issue, should worry about what the majority's claim of power portends" (8).

"I Just Want to Hear the Gospel"

I have heard people who suffer from same-sex attraction say, "I just want to hear the Gospel." In the midst of all the political and legal fights to justify homosexual marriage and protect (or perhaps promote) homosexual rights, real people with real struggles are being lost. Christians dare not let their frustrations and disappointments with the failures of their political leaders distract them from the reality that there are real individuals around them who struggle against homosexual feelings. They are people who are pouring themselves out to God with repentant hearts and who are in need of hearing that Jesus loves them. Unfortunately, there are Christians who take their frustrations out on people needing grace. Instead of words of consolation, they pile on curses. Those who are already convicted by the law and feel their sins do not need more law. They need to hear that Jesus loves them in their weakness and that He died to forgive them all their sins. Even persistent sins of struggling with forbidden urges were taken up into the love and grace of Christ and pardoned at the cross.

When I was a kid in confirmation class, my pastor wrote the numbers of the commandments on a chalkboard from 1 to 10. When he got to the Sixth Commandment, "Thou shalt not commit adultery," he wrote the number 6 about four times larger than all the other numbers. "That," he said, "is how many Christians look at sexual sins." He was right. In high school, I watched as a girl who got pregnant was ridiculed by adults for her "terrible immorality," while those same adults did not seem to care that their own kids were having premarital sex. Curiously, they also seemed oblivious to the fact that there was a boy who got her pregnant and who was just as guilty as she was. Those whose sexual sins are out in the open become targets for those who remain blind to their own sin.

It is worse for men and women who suffer from same-sex attraction. There is a kind of heterosexual double standard that shows revulsion at the very mention of homosexual attraction but then thinks nothing of its own lust for the opposite sex. This is a double standard that is noticed and marked by people who suffer from same-sex attraction. It makes them hesitant to seek help in the Church. It was discussed earlier how important it is that people who struggle with sexual sins know with certainty that the Church will be a place of refuge for them. When church-going Christians treat them poorly, the effects are more devastating than if non-churchgoers had belittled them.

People suffering under the weight of their sins, no matter what those sins are, need a place of safety where they will not be attacked. They need a community of loving people who will stand at their side and confess their own sins without measuring whose sin is biggest. They do not need a permissive attitude that does not care what they do or who they are. They need an atmosphere of honesty where each person looks first to the log in his or her own eye before worrying about the speck in his or her brother's or sister's eye. Church-going people need to be reminded that the sins of the pious senior citizen who likes to gossip a bit are just as much in need of repentance and forgiveness as the sins of the street walking prostitute; the sins of the heterosexual are just as damnable as those of the homosexual. Once repented, all sins are treated the same by God— they are forgiven and washed away as if they never happened.

Jesus repeatedly sought out those trapped in sexual sins and announced the forgiving love of God to them. He shocked the good moral people of the world more than once by treating sexual immorality with kindness and compassion, not rebuking but forgiving. In Luke 7, when Jesus was in the house of an upstanding Pharisee, a "woman of the city" came uninvited to Jesus. She cried so much at His feet that they were soaked with her tears. She dried them with her hair and then poured a costly perfume on them, which was probably purchased with the money she made selling her body on the street. The same hands that handled the private parts of other men touched the feet of Jesus. It was more than the good Pharisee could stand. In his heart, he thought to himself, "If this man were a prophet, He would have known who and what sort of woman this is who is touching Him, for she is a sinner" (Luke 7:39). Her sexual sins were so gross and so public that his sense of holiness was offended at her. But Jesus was not offended because of her sins. He welcomed her broken heart and received her repentance. When no one else would say a kind word to this woman, Jesus looked her in the eye and said, "Your sins are forgiven. . . .Your faith has saved you; go in peace" (Luke 7:48, 50). Her faith certainly was not strong enough previously to keep her from a life of sexual perversion, but even in her immorality, the Holy Spirit found her and drew her to her Savior. In that moment, as she knelt before the Son of God, the full weight of her sins came pouring out. She knew that Jesus saw the whole horrible story of her life. Every unspeakable act she committed with other men was on display in front of the all-knowing gaze of Christ. She was broken by it and deeply sorry for it. Jesus' response to her repentance was to show her the kind of love that no one else would. He put away any thoughts of condemnation toward her. He forgave her and spoke therapeutic words of reconciliation to her.

This is the same way Jesus treated the young woman caught in adultery in John 8. When a crowd of men wanted to stone her for adultery, Jesus reminded them that they were no less sinners. "Let him who is without sin among you be the first to throw a stone at her" (John 8:7). Then Jesus told her that He did not condemn her. There was forgiveness with Him. The young woman would not have to answer for her adultery because Jesus had taken it into Himself and would pay for her sin along with the sins of the rest of the world. Jesus did not write the Sixth Commandment with an extra-large 6.

Christians do not weigh forgiveness according to what sin a person has committed. When sinners show sorrow over sin and seek love and grace from Christ, then the role of the Christian is to tell them that Jesus does love them and has forgiven their sins. Those who see that their attractions and desires are contrary to God's will and who look to Christ for mercy to help should be told plainly and without hesitation that Jesus loves them. Jesus died for the sins of the world. He bore their sins for them so they would not have to face God's wrath. And by that forgiveness, Jesus will strengthen them, bless them with His Spirit, and help them overcome temptation.

In no sense does this mean that Christians should ignore the nature of homosexuality as sin or deny the severe damage it can do to the soul. The Christian faith demands that when we encounter those who insist on their right to be homosexual and who try to defend their same-sex attractions as acceptable to God, we must make clear to them that God does not bless what His Word forbids. On the contrary, God clearly condemns homosexuality as He does every other form of lust and sexual activity outside of marriage. God will judge those who choose to ignore His Word and turn away from His truth. To those who live in unrepentance and defend their right to disobey God, we must speak His law and help them understand the seriousness of rejecting the purity of Christ.

For the many thousands of men, women, and adolescents who are repentant and who struggle with their flesh, the Church is Christ's answer. It is God's will that no one should perish but that all come to repentance (2 Peter 3:9). The absolution God gives those who are repentant is not a feeling people get through pious thoughts. It is an actual word of forgiveness spoken into the ears of hurting sinners. Through a mere word, God created the heavens and the earth; and through a word of pardon, God recreates people in Christ's image. Sins against God's gift of sex, whether they are sinful thoughts or sinful actions, find reconciliation in the gifts of grace Christ gives out in His Church. His Word will not return to Him void, but will accomplish what pleases Him (Isaiah 55:11). And nothing pleases God more than washing people clean from sin and giving them life in His Son.

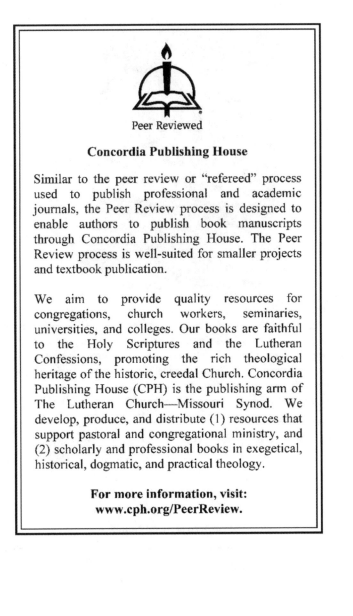

Peer Reviewed

Concordia Publishing House

Similar to the peer review or "refereed" process used to publish professional and academic journals, the Peer Review process is designed to enable authors to publish book manuscripts through Concordia Publishing House. The Peer Review process is well-suited for smaller projects and textbook publication.

We aim to provide quality resources for congregations, church workers, seminaries, universities, and colleges. Our books are faithful to the Holy Scriptures and the Lutheran Confessions, promoting the rich theological heritage of the historic, creedal Church. Concordia Publishing House (CPH) is the publishing arm of The Lutheran Church—Missouri Synod. We develop, produce, and distribute (1) resources that support pastoral and congregational ministry, and (2) scholarly and professional books in exegetical, historical, dogmatic, and practical theology.

**For more information, visit:
www.cph.org/PeerReview.**

A Guide for the Christian Family

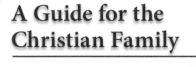

Learning About Sex

An honest, Christian approach to the body, relationships, and sex.

From preschoolers to adults, the Learning about Sex series makes the awesome gift of sexuality understandable. Age-appropriate language and graphics throughout the six books help children recognize gender differences as one of God's great gifts designed as part of His creative plan.

✳ ✳ ✳

Get articles, videos, and much more at cph.org/las.

Concordia
Publishing House